MW01173537

CONCRETE WALLS AND STEEL BARS

For information about the book, contact:

Twitter: @concretewalls1
Instagram: Concretewallsandsteelbars
Facebook: Phillip D White
Email: Concretewallsandsteelbars@Gmail.com
Email: AllmoneyEmpire@Gmail.com

Published By: All Money Empire, LLC

ISBN:

Book Cover Design by:

Printed in the United States of America by:

Concrete Walls & Steel Bars – "The New Willie Lynch"

Table of Contents

Acknowledgments

First and foremost, I would like to take the time to thank God Almighty. Through all my adversity, struggles, trials and tribulations, He walked with me. And when I was too weary to carry on, He carried me. Thank you to my Lord and Savior.

I would like to thank my beautiful mother who taught me to never allow negativity to control my thought processes and to continue to make my situation work for me. Thank you Queen. I would like to thank my father for giving me life and dropping jewels onto me. To my stepfather, thank you. You did what most "men" wouldn't do.

My grandmother, you are truly the sunshine that shines down on me. You warned me that the world would evolve into a place where people cherished manmade things instead of nature and life. I guess you were right. Let's see if this book can change that. I love you. For my grandmother who received her wings in 2010 and is now with the Lord, smiling down on me, thank you for always believing in me. I'll love you for life and save me a plate! To my grandpa and uncle that passed away, I love you both.

Last but not least, to my kids; my beautiful rays of hope. I love the three of you dearly. Words alone can't compensate for my absence and the void I've left in your lives. I love you. I'm changing for the better because of the three of you, so that no other child has to go through life fatherless. I've experienced the reality of having a "father" whom I wish was there, but wasn't. I also experienced having a father-figure who didn't have to be there, but was. But eventually, I still ended up raising myself at 12 years old.

To my lovely sister, you know you are the missing puzzle to my life. You are the inspiration that ignites my fire. To my little brother, you know what it is; I love you brah. Let God guide you. To my uncle who came to my trial, I love you.

I want to take this time to apologize to the victims of my actions and crimes; the families I destroyed with my past negative lifestyle; the communities and neighborhoods I destroyed with the poison I distributed; the reckless genocide I took part in; and the negative influences that I had on the younger generation which looked up to me, my deepest and sincere apologies.

I dedicate this book to the innocent lives lost and innocent blood shed for the love of money, cars, clothes and material possessions. You did not die in vain. I carry the torch for you. This book is dedicated to anyone I hurt, wronged, caused pain, or disrupted in a negative way. I apologize. I give to you a new person with insight and remorse for his wrongs. This book is dedicated to you, your family and your future. I make no excuses. I'm growing and developing into a mature adult who now holds himself accountable for his actions. Please know I love you. God is good and He has forgiven me. I ask for your forgiveness, too.

I want to take this time to salute my brother, sister, both of my children's mothers and my cousins. Y'all know who y'all are. Also, I thank my brother-in-law, my lil cuz (my protégé who allows me to breathe through him), my aunties and my uncles; and to my real partners in Naptown, 765 Muncie, Anderson, Indiana, Atlanta and California. To my Lil' brah fighting them Feds, chin up…chest out… To my big cuz who got my typewriter, thank you. Good investment, huh? ☺ To my uncle who taught me the hustle, love you, unc.

Let me give a chin-up, chest-out to all the political prisoners and convicts who wake up daily with ambition to change for the better; to pay their debts to the ones they've wronged by educating themselves; and to mold and lace the younger generation with knowledge and wisdom to be better than they were. We can't change the past but we can write our future. Make everyday count. Do something productive with your life and when you leave they can trace your legacy for others to follow. This is just the beginning of something beautiful. There will be more books added to the "*Concrete Walls and Steel Barz*" series. I can't wait to see you all on the other side of the cell. From me to you: chin-up, chest-out. I love you all.

Yours Truly,

Bulletproof love,

Mr. P. D. White

P. S.

I purposely chose to leave the names of family and friends out of this book. You deserve the right to have your name and privacy protected and not become the subject of any criticism for my past negative actions. I also have too many to name and it would take a lot of pages… There is no other…!!!

Dedication

This book is dedicated to all the communities around the globe.

It's better to have peace than to be divided into pieces.

For my children, may this book rewrite my legacy

and provide you with true insight. I love you.

Foreword

I met Phillip White when I became his defense attorney, appointed by the California Courts to represent him in an appeal that we have taken to the Supreme Court. It is with some surprise, and much admiration, that I sit here now, introducing a compelling book that Phillip has written from a prison cell, accomplishing against steep odds and great adversity, a meaningful and insightful literary work.

In some ways, Phillip's situation is like many of my clients: he is a black man who is dealing with the California Prison System, and all its ramifications, from the inside. However, in a lot of other fundamental ways, Phillip White is a unique individual. And I have been honored to experience that uniqueness: a singular ability to be positive and creative and to always be absolutely real while existing inside a system that fosters none of those attributes. This is because those attributes come from within Phillip White, and they emanate outward. They touch those who are close to him, and they bring enlightenment in and about a system where there would otherwise be ignorance.

This book shows this, and in this book he shares that experience. It is, ultimately, about possibilities: the possibility of being positive in the face of overwhelming negativity, of seeking enlightenment rather than succumbing to rage, struggling endlessly against adversity in many forms, while also seeing the humor, beauty and grace in God's gifts.

As the author of this work, Phillip explains critical elements of our current society, and indeed our history, as only one who has actually lived at the heart of those elements can explain: how the prison system operates as a mode of modern day slavery; how education is the antidote to that systemic repression; and how all of this intersects with public policy, politics, and in the end, with reality itself in the most profound and sublime sense. Positivity, creativity and light can replace systemic repression and self-destructive behavior by the victims of that system. Mr. White shows us a way to understand this, and most importantly, to change it both from within and from without.

Defense Criminal Attorney at Law
Mr. Geoffrey Jones, Esq.
Fairfax, CA 94930

Ignorant

By Mr. P.D. White

One thing I can't stand is a Nigga –

Not a Nigger, N-i-g-g-e-r, but a Nigga…

And let's be clear, when I say nigga, I'm not addressing the

brother of color who had to hustle to support his mother,

sister and little brother;

Trying to show them affection and let them know

we had each other's back like backpacks

with straps which continue to fall off our shoulders

when the weight of the world begins to feel like boulders.

I'm not talking down on the brother who sits at the bus stop

on his way to work with his Beats® by Dr. Dre headphones

on,

rapping out loud because today is payday and he's just happy

when he screamed, "Mayday, Mayday," God made an

attempt

to prevent his crash landing — that was destined to happen.

Nawl…when I say I can't stand a nigga, I mean just that…a nigga.

One who knows the cards are stacked against us,

But still sits at the poker table of life full of card sharks yelling, "Deal!"

Taking himself further into debt while dragging his family and friends with him…

like they signed up for this bullshit…

"Once again we gots to take our hard earned money and bail ol' Leroy out of jail

cause instead of cutting Mrs. Jones yard for $10 he decided to break in her house…

stole her lil' black and white TV…wasn't worth more than $5."

"We all told Ronda to keep her legs closed, but she scoffed at us.

Decided to open her home to young trap stars and gang members

Who sold dope out her front door and stashed them big ol' guns by her back door…

Task raided her house, took her black ass to jail.

Took her kids to CPS, took her Section 8, but guess who she
called from jail?

Sure wasn't Teddy, Big Smoke and Tiny Loc.

Shit! They bonded out and moved on to the next Nigga's
house."

Nigga, don't look at me sideways when I say it. We all let
it roll off our tongues like the tears that rolled down
the faces of them poor black folks who fought hard
not to be called Niggers!

When I say nigga, I'm talking about those who define
negativity
so much that if you looked up the word you'd probably see
their face in place of it. I'm talking about the brother, excuse
me
nigga, nigga, that shot yo nigga; the one who claim he did it
because he was not yo nigga.

The nigga who ran like a coward and forgot yo nigga — was
his brother.

Another black man cursed by the color of his skin
which to most is a blessing and a sin, a gift and a curse.

Excuse me if I sound as if I'm in church…but they got niggas in there chasing skirts;

niggas dressed as preachers — blood suckers and leachers —

fake prophets and teachers; running game with education but still can't teach us;

Claiming to have the cleansing holy water but still can't bleach us.

Nigga!! Get yo hands out of my pocket!

They "claim" it was a nigga that killed Malcolm…

wait…let me stop it.

I know niggas who work all week and take that paycheck and start tricking;

Instead of providing for his family he throws it at the nigga stripping .

I know niggas who owe child support that ain't paid one red digit;

At the weed house talking 'bout, "Roll that blunt nigga so I can hit it."

I know niggas who look down on other brothers,

but their courage is as short as midgets.

On the stand in the courtroom yelling out, "Of course that nigga did it!"

The New Willie Lynch   Concrete Walls & Steel Bars
Mr. P. D. White

That's the nigga that I hate; that's the nigga I can't stand…

You don't have to be an African King or Queen,

Just be a real woman or a real man.

Now they say Jesus was black, fact is he just might be;

But I bet a nigga say, "How the fuck is that Jesus

and he looks just like you and me?"

Exactly — a Nigga is spelled I-G-N-O-R-A-N-T!

Introduction

Willie Lynch

The Making of a Slave

This speech was delivered by Willie Lynch on the bank of the James River in the colony of Virginia in 1712. Lynch was a British slave owner in the West Indies. He was invited to the colony of Virginia in 1712 to teach his methods to slave owners there. The term, "lynching" is derived from his last name. Other research study indicates the term "lynching" is derived from a native of Virginia named Charles Lynch. The authenticity of the Willie Lynch letters has been the topic of many discussions. Some say it's a myth; some say it's real. Regardless of its history, it's relevant.

GREETINGS

"Gentlemen, I greet you here on the bank of the James River in the year of our Lord one thousand seven hundred and twelve. First, I shall thank you, the gentlemen of the Colony of Virginia, for bringing me here. I am here to help you solve some of your problems with slaves. Your invitation reached me on my modest plantation in the West Indies where I experimented with some of the newest, and still some of the oldest, methods for control of slaves. Ancient Romans would envy us if my program is implemented.

As our boat sailed south on the James River, named for our illustrious King whose version of the Bible we cherish, I saw enough to know that your problem is not unique. While Rome used cords of wood crosses for standing human bodies along its highway in great numbers, you are here using the tree and the rope on occasion. I caught the whiff of a dead slave hanging from a tree a couple of miles back. You are not only losing valuable stock by hangings; you are having uprisings; your slaves are running away; you suffer occasional fires; your animals are killed; and your crops are sometimes left in the fields too long for maximum profit.

Gentlemen, do you know what your problems are? I do not need to elaborate. I am not here to enumerate your problems, but to introduce you to a method of solving them. In my bag here, I have a fool-proof method for controlling your black slaves. I guarantee you if implemented correctly it will control the slaves for at least 300 years. My method is simple: Any member of your family or your overseer can use it. I have outlined a number of differences among the slaves. Then I take these differences and make them bigger. I use fear, distrust and envy for control purposes. These methods have worked on my modest plantation in the West Indies and it will work throughout the South.

Take this simple little list of differences and think about them. At the top of my list is "*Age*" but it's only there because it starts with the letter "*A*." The second is "*Color*" or shade. The others are: *Intelligence*, *Size* and *Sex*; *Size* of the *Plantations*; their *Status* on the plantations; *Attitude* of the owners; whether the slaves live in the valley, on a hill, east, west, north or south; and whether they have fine or coarse hair and are short or tall. Now that you have a list of differences, I shall give you an outline of action. But, before I do that, I shall assure you that *Distrust* is stronger than *Trust*, and *Envy* stronger than *Adulation*, *Respect* or *Admiration*.

After receiving this indoctrination, the black slaves shall carry on and become self-fueling and self-generating for hundreds of years, maybe thousands. Don't forget, you must pit the *Old* black male against the *Young* black male, and the *Young* black male against the *Old* black male. You must use the *Dark-skinned* slaves vs. the *Light-skinned* slaves, and the *Light-skinned* slaves vs. the *Dark-skinned* slaves. You must use the *Female* vs. the *Male*, and the *Male* vs. the *Female*. You must also have your white servants and overseers distrust all blacks. However, it is necessary that your slaves *Trust* and *Depend* on *Us*. They must *Love*, *Respect* and *Trust* only *Us*.

Gentlemen, these kits are your keys to control. Use them. Have your wives and children use them. Never miss an opportunity to do so. *The Slaves Themselves Will Remain Perpetually Distrustful If These Methods Are Used Intensely For One Year.* Gentlemen, thank you."

LET'S MAKE A SLAVE

It was the interest and business of slave holders to study human nature—and the slave nature in particular—with a view to practical results. I, and many of them, attained astonishing proficiency in this direction. They had to deal not with earth, wood and stone, but with men. And by every regard they had for their own safety and prosperity, they needed to know the material on which they were to work. Knowing what they themselves would do, they were conscious of the injustice and wrongs they were perpetuating every hour. Were they the victims of such wrongs? They were constantly looking for the first signs of the dreaded retribution.

Therefore, they watched with skilled and practiced eyes and learned to read, with great accuracy, the state of mind and heart of the slave through his sable face. If a slave displayed unusual sobriety, apparent abstractions, sullenness and indifference; indeed any mood out of common was afforded ground for suspicion and inquiry.

Frederick Douglas' *Let's Make a Slave* is a study of the scientific process of man-breaking and slave-making. It describes the rationale and results of the Anglo-Saxon's ideas and methods of insuring the master/slave relationship. *Let's Make a Slave: The Original and Development of a Social Being Called "The Negro."*

So, let us make a slave. What do we need? First, we need a black nigger man, a pregnant nigger woman and her baby nigger boy. Secondly, we will use the same basic principles we use when breaking a horse, combined with some more sustaining factors. What we do with horses is break them away from one form of life to another, that is, we reduce them from their natural state in nature. Whereas nature provides them with the natural capacity to take care of their offspring, we break their natural string of independence and thereby create a dependency state of being. Then we are able to get from them useful production for our business and pleasure.

CARDINAL PRINCIPLES FOR MAKING A NEGRO

These strategies were developed for fear that our future generations would not understand the principles of breaking both beasts together: the nigger and the horse. We understand that short-range planning economics results in periodic economic chaos. However, to avoid turmoil in the economy, it requires us to have breadth and depth in long-range comprehensive planning, articulating both skill and sharp perceptions.   Therefore, we lay down the following principles for long-range comprehensive economic planning.

Both horse and nigger are no good to the economy in their wild or natural state. Both must be *broken* and *tied* together for orderly production. For an orderly future, special and particular attention must be paid to the *female* and the *youngest* offspring. Both must be *crossbred* to produce a variety and division of labor.

Both must be taught to respond to a peculiar new *language.* Psychological and physical instruction of *containment* must be created for both.

We hold the six cardinal principles as truth to be self-evident based upon the following discourse concerning the economics of breaking and tying the horse and the nigger together; all inclusive of the six principles laid down. NOTE: Neither principle alone will suffice for good economics. All principles must be employed for the orderly good of the nation. Accordingly, both a wild horse and a wild or natural nigger are dangerous, even if captured. They will have the tendency to seek their customary freedom and might kill you in your sleep. You cannot rest. They sleep while you are awake and are awake when you are sleep. They are *dangerous* near the family house and it requires too much labor to watch them away from the house. Most of all, you cannot get them to work in this natural state. Therefore, the horse and the nigger must be broken; that is, breaking them from one form of mental state to another. *Keep the body but take the mind!* In other words, break the will to resist.

Now the breaking process is the same, by slightly varying degrees, for both the horse and the nigger. But, as we said before, there is an art to long-range planning. *You must keep your eye and thoughts on the female* and the *offspring* of the horse and the nigger. A brief discourse in offspring development will shed light on the key to sound economic principles. Pay little attention to the generation of original breaking. You must *concentrate on future generations*. And, if you *break* the *female* mother, she will break the offspring in its early years of development therefore, when her offspring is old enough to work, she will deliver it up to you because her normal female protective tendencies will have been lost in the original breaking process.

For example, take the case of the wild stud horse, a female horse and an infant horse and compare the breaking process with two captured nigger males in their natural state and a pregnant nigger woman with her infant offspring. Take the stud horse and break him for limited containment. Completely break the female horse until she becomes very gentle and you ar anybody can ride her in comfort. Breed the mare and the stud until you have the desired offspring. Then you can return the stud to freedom until you need him again. Train the female horse to the point where she will eat out of your hand and, in return, she will also train the infant horse to eat out of your hand.

When it comes to breaking the uncivilized nigger use the same process but vary the degree and step up the pressure in order to perform a complete reversal of mind. Take the meanest and most restless nigger and strip him of his clothing in front of the remaining male niggers, the female and her nigger infant. Next, tar and feather him, tying each of his legs to a different horse faced in opposite directions. Then you set him afire and beat both horses to get them to pull him apart in front of the remaining niggers.

Finally, you take a bullwhip and beat the remaining male niggers to the point of death in front of the female and infant. Don't kill them, but *put the fear of God in them* so they can be useful for future breeding.

THE BREAKING PROCESS OF THE AFRICAN AMERICAN WOMAN

Take the female and run a series of tests on her to see if she will submit to your desires willingly. Test her in every way because she is the most important factor for good economics. If she shows any signs of resistance to submitting completely to your will, do not hesitate to use the bullwhip on her to extract that last bit of bitch out of her. Take care not to kill her because in doing so you spoil good economics. When she has completely submitted she will train her offspring in their early years to submit to labor when they become of age. Understanding is the most important thing. Therefore we shall delve deeper into the subject matter concerning what is produced as a result of the breaking process of the female nigger.

We have reversed the relationship in her natural uncivilized state. Normally she would have strong dependency on the uncivilized nigger male. But now, she has a limited protective tendency toward her independent male offspring and will raise them to be dependent like her. Nature has provided for this type of balance. We reversed nature by burning and pulling a civilized nigger apart and bullwhipping the others to the point of death in the female's presence. With her being alone, unprotected and the *male image destroyed*, the ordeal caused her to move from her psychologically dependent state to a frozen independent state. In this frozen state of psychological independence she will raise her *male* and female offspring in reversed roles. Out of *fear* of the young male's life she will psychologically train him to be *mentally weak* and *dependent*, but *physically strong*.

Because she has become psychologically independent, she will train her *female* offspring to be psychologically independent. So what have you got? You've got the *nigger woman out front and the nigger man behind her and scared*. This is a perfect situation for sound sleep and sound economics. Before the breaking process, we had to be alert and on guard at all times. Now we can sleep soundly because out of frozen fear the female stands guard for us. The male can't get past her early slave-molding process. He has become a good tool, now ready to be tied to the horse at a tender age. So by the time a nigger boy reaches the age of sixteen, he is soundly broken in and ready for a long life of sound and efficient work; the reproduction of a unit of good labor force.

We have created an orbiting cycle that turns on its own axis forever by the continual breaking of uncivilized savage niggers; by throwing the nigger female savage into a psychological state of independence; by killing the protective male image; and by creating a submissive dependent mind of the nigger male slave. This will continue unless a phenomenon occurs and re-shifts the position of the male and female slaves. Let's show what we mean by example. Take the case of the two economic slave units and let's examine them closely.

THE NEGRO MARRIAGE UNIT

We breed two nigger males with two nigger females. Then we take the nigger males away from them and keep them moving and working. Let's say one nigger female a nigger female and the other bears a nigger male. Both nigger females, being without the influence of the nigger male image and frozen in a psychological state of independence, will raise their offspring in reverse positions. The one with the nigger female offspring will teach her to be like herself: independent and negotiable (we negotiate with her, through her, by her and at will). The one with the nigger male offspring, in subconscious fear for his life, will raise him to be mentally dependent and weak but physically strong; in other words, body over mind.   Then in a few years when these two offspring become fertile for early reproduction, we will mate and breed them and continue the cycle. That is good, sound and long-range comprehensive planning.

WARNING: POSSIBLE INTERLOPING NEGATIVES

Earlier we talked about the noneconomic good of the horse and nigger in their wild or natural state; discussed the principle of breaking and tying them together for orderly production. Furthermore, we talked about paying particular attention to the female savage and her offspring for orderly future planning. Then more recently we stated that by reversing the positions of the male and female savages, we created an orbiting cycle that turns on its own axis unless a phenomenon occur and re-shifts the male and female savages' positions. Our experts have warned us about the possibility of this phenomenon occurring because the mind has a strong drive to correct and re-correct itself over a period of time if it touches some substantial original historical base. They advised us that the best way to deal with the phenomenon is to shave off the brute's mental history and create a multiplicity of phenomena of illusions. Therefore, each illusion will twirl on its own orbit, similar to floating balls in a vacuum.

This creation of a multiplicity of phenomena of illusions entails the principle of crossbreeding the nigger and the horse as we stated above. The purpose is to create a diversified division of labor thereby creating different levels of labor and different values of illusion at each connecting level of labor. This will result in the severance of the points of original beginnings for each sphere illusion. Since we feel that the subject matter may get more complicated as we proceed in outlining our economic plan concerning the purpose, reason and effect of crossbreeding horses and niggers, we shall share this definition of terms for future generations:

1. Orbiting cycle - a thing turning in a given path.

2. Axis – that upon which or around which a body turns.

3. Phenomenon - something beyond ordinary conception and inspires awe and wonder.

4. Multiplicity – a great number.

5. Sphere – means a globe

6. Crossbreeding a Horse – taking a horse and breeding it with an ass and you get a dumb, backward ass and long-headed mule that is not reproductive or productive by itself.

7. Crossbreeding niggers – taking so many drops of good, white blood and injecting them into as many nigger women as possible, varying the number of drops dependent upon what skin tone you want. Then you let them breed with each other until a circle of new colors you desire appear.

What this means is this: Put the niggers and the horse in a breeding pot along with some asses and good, white blood; mix them together and what do you get? You get a multiplicity of colors of ass-backwards, unusual niggers running, tied to backward ass, long-headed mules; one productive of itself and the other sterile (the one constant, the other dying. We keep the nigger constant because we may replace the mules with another tool). The mule and the nigger were tied to each other, neither knowing where the other had come from and neither productive by itself or without each other.

CONTROLLED LANGUAGE

After crossbreeding is completed, for further severance from their original beginning, *we must completely annihilate the mother tongue* of both the new nigger and the new mule. We must institute a new language that involves the new life-work of both. You know, language is peculiar institution. It leads to the heart of a people. The more a foreigner knows about the language of another the more he is able to move through all levels of that society. Therefore, if the foreigner is an enemy of that country, to the extent that he knows the body of the language, is the extent to which the country is vulnerable to attack or invasion by that foreign culture.

For example, if you take a slave and teach him all about your language he will know all your secrets. Then he is no longer a slave because you can't fool him any longer. *Being a fool is one of the basic ingredients to the maintenance of the slavery system.* For example, if you told a slave that he must perform in getting out "our crops" and he knows the language well, he would know that "our crops" didn't mean "his crops, too" and the slavery system would break down because he would understand the command on the basis of what "our crops" really meant. So you must be careful when setting up the new language for the slaves or the new slaves in your house will be talking to you as "man to man" and that will be death to our economic system.

In addition, the definitions of words or terms are only a minute part of the process. Values are created and transported by communication through the body of language. A total society has many interconnected value systems. All the values in the society have bridges of language to connect them for orderly working in the society. However, if not for these language bridges, the many value systems would sharply clash and cause internal strife or civil war; the degree of the conflict being determined by the magnitude of the issues or relative opposing strength in whatever form.

For example, if you put a slave in a pig pen and train him to live there and incorporate in him to value it as a complete way of life, the biggest problem you would have out of him is that he would worry you about provisions to keep the pig pen clean. However, if you make a slip and incorporate something into his language whereby he comes to value a house more than he does his pig pen, you got a problem. He will soon be in your house.

* * * * * * * * * * * * * *

It is important to note that this "Letter" was brought to my attention around 2001 through many pamphlets, news articles, social media websites and wise, older men who enlightened me about its existence. After further research, I discovered there is also a history linking Virginia native Charles Lynch to the term "lynching" from which it is said the term is derived from his last name.

The New Willie Lynch
By Mr. P.D. White

<u>TRUTH REVEALED</u>

This is the first time I can honestly say I appreciate the "Willie Lynch Letters" guide about how to make a slave, break a slave and keep a slave. In 1712, he told slave owners "if you follow my instructions you will have the Negro under your control for the next 300 years." So let's fast forward and it is over 300 years since his "famous predictions." He must have been some type of psychic or fortune teller because not only was he precise and correct, but our way of thinking is too far gone and it is time for us to put those white sheets on ourselves. Shit, we are no different than the K.K.K. The word "nigga" is so popular it has become a fashion statement, a trend, a way of life. It's become cool for Mexicans, whites, Asians and other races to use it. Those marches Martin Luther King Jr. marched in were in vain. Now we are marching down your mother's street with military-issue, high-powered rifles, killing any and everything in our way. Even the cats, dogs and vacant vehicles aren't safe! The Willie Lynch — ha ha!!! I laugh. This individual actually told the truth!

The late great 2Pac (Tupac Shakur) said it perfectly: "**IT'S NOT THEM KILLING US; IT'S US KILLING US...IT'S NOT**

31

THEM KNOCKING US OFF; IT'S US KNOCKING US OFF!!" ("MAKAVELI" in this white man's world). I remember reading a book called *"From Niggas to Gods"* and it talked about the term "Niggativity." Yeah, we're still making lame excuses such as "it's their fault," or "because of them I can't do this or that" …yeah. This may be true, but what do you do with your profits you make after you poison your own community and people with drugs, prostitution and genocide? Oh, do you not give it right back to "them," the same ones you blame for holding you back— racism and oppression? "You got gold all in your chain, gold all in your rang, gold all in your watch. You got to have Gucci, Louie, Coogi, Fendi, Prada. You got to have money, clothes, cars, and hoes…cause that's all that my niggas know."

Let's take a moment to reflect on the most serious issues society has dealt with in the past five years: We have seen and witnessed the death of Oscar Grant, an unarmed black man who was shot in cold blood by a transit rent-a-cop. We've sat back and watched the trial of George Zimmerman and his acquittal for the murder of an unarmed black teenager, Trayvon Martin. We've sat glued to our televisions as we anxiously awaited grand jury decisions, in both Ferguson, Missouri and New York City, surrounding the unlawful murder of Michael Brown, another unarmed teen murdered in cold blood by a psychopathic police officer; as well as an unarmed black man who was choked to death by police officers who applied tactics and takedown strategies as if the poor father and husband was a U. F. C. opponent and not a working, taxpaying citizen who had no criminal record or hadn't committed any crime that lead to his death.

America has become so deranged with the black community and our trends that our children can no longer ride around town with their music blasting and windows rolled down because we all remember what happened in Florida at the gas station when an ignorant white adult decided to be a noise pollution officer. He not only brandished a firearm at four unarmed teenagers but also opened fire into the vehicle, killing one and injuring the others. So the question is, "When do we educate our youth and community on morals, conduct, integrity and character?" Of course we should have no dress codes. Hell, our kids should be able to wear whatever they choose to wear without being targeted. Our children should be able to play their music as loud as they choose. Our children shouldn't be harassed by officers for being black!

But our children should also know and understand that it is a setup. This setup has been put in motion for hundreds of years before our time. How we conduct ourselves and carry ourselves is a reflection on the black culture as a whole. Where is the unity? Where is the communication? Where is the guidance that we once saw in the early 50's, 60's and 70's? Where are the family morals? If we take a good look at ourselves in the mirror and ask ourselves, "What do I value the most in life?" most of our answers would fall very short of reality. Below is a list of things that are valued in America based on a survey which looks at black incarcerated men from 18 to 60 years of age:

1. Money
2. Stability/Financial Security
3. Image/Reputation
4. Mother
5. God
6. Children (for those who had children)

What do you see wrong with this list? And by the way, the topics are listed in the correct order based on the survey taken. God was valued 2nd to last and the ruler of all evil, money, placed first. We may become judgmental and say "this is just stupid" or "whoever values money over everything is dumb," but when you listen to the radio or turn on the television this is all you hear and see: "Money over everything (M.O.E.)" or "Money over bitches." So a lot of the brothers who participated in this survey fell victim to this way of life and were programmed with this way of thinking. Our community doesn't respect those hardworking individuals anymore. We glorify murder, drugs, pimping, prostitution and gangs, and we look down on those who want to go to college or who want to be doctors, lawyers, scientists, police officers (those who are serious about protecting the community and being an asset for the community), etc. If you aren't pushing a candy-coated car on 28-inch wheels which cost you $15,000, you are looked at as "being in the way." If you don't involve yourself with negative folks, drug usage or gang activity you are frowned upon and looked at as being a square, soft, or even a sellout! This is how backwards our way of thinking is; this is what Willie Lynch embedded in our minds and tribes over 300 years ago. And guess what? **IT'S STILL WORKING TODAY!!!** It's sad. Not only are we blinded, we are allowing ourselves to be hoodwinked.

A lot of us do know what's going on and we just don't care. In this book you will be brought a little closer to the dark side and reality. I will give you the facts and no opinions. I will open your eyes to the nightmares and shattered dreams of the average black teen growing up in this corrupt society. If this book is studied and not just read, then and only then can we begin to reverse the Willie Lynch syndrome. I'm not going to complain or fill up 200 pages telling you what you did wrong or what you didn't do right. I'm going to share with you the key to reprogramming your way of thinking, raising your children and communicating with not only those of your same race but those outside of the black community. Are you ready for change? Are you ready to take a trip into reality? Are you ready to live a productive, peaceful, happy life where you don't have to feel paranoid and look over your shoulder? Well you've made the first step by picking up this book.

Now I could get on some wild beautiful black sister hype and preach about how precious your mind, body and spirit is. But the truth of the matter is would you listen? Do you even care? So

I'm just going to "keep it real" like most of these brothers claim to keep it.   Truth of the matter is the average black queen isn't searching for a king, a real man, a real father to his children.   They would rather cheat themselves and settle for less.   Let's be honest. If Jesus himself came to earth and presented himself as the Son of God and the woman had all the proof that she needed that it was Him, nine times out of ten the lost woman would choose the man on 28-inch rims, wearing 2 chains, with an iced-out Jesus piece around his neck before she would choose to walk with Jesus. Some of our Queens want to twerk, pop mollies, drink champagne and be showered with dead presidents for degrading themselves. The new way of thinking is, "I'm gone shake this ass for some cash."   Then what happens?   Her son no longer respects her or women; and her daughter becomes enticed and mesmerized by the dollars her mother brings in, the clothes she wears and the dance moves she makes around the house while watching B.E.T., the most dominant black cable channel in the world, which glorifies murder, drugs, violence and genocide in the black communities.

Let me back up a few steps and enlighten you on a few things.   I'm not pro-black and I'm not anti-white.   I'm not even on a journey back to Africa but I am wise and wide awake now.   For so long I was blind, lost and fell victim to being hoodwinked by the same people I considered my family and friends.   It wasn't until I started looking at myself in the mirror and questioning my own actions and ulterior motives that I realized I was also to blame. Yeah, big ol' Phil. I'm at fault. When I first started selling cocaine and weed in 1992 (at age12), it was for one purpose and one purpose only: to help my mother with the bills and put food on the table for my younger sister and brother. Once I learned how easy it was to hustle to pay the bills and buy the things I liked in life such as shoes, clothes, jewelry, liquor, more weed to smoke, vehicles, etc., I no longer hustled to survive or keep my family's head above the water. Now I was hustling to shine. In other words to stunt, flex and showboat. Now that I'm older and wiser I realized that in order for me to have that car on rims, $300.00 pairs of shoes, nice furniture in my home and nice clothes on my kids back, I had to poison my own community, my own folks, my "brothers and sisters" who were struggling just like me. I took advantage of another person's weakness in order for me to gain financial and material strength. I was selfish. I had fallen victim to the "Willie Lynch Syndrome."

If we look around and observe our surroundings what do we see? The exact same formula I explained to you, the exact same lifestyle. Some poor fatherless child forced into the game at an early age, just trying to make it, just trying to survive. In the beginning he has good intentions, but after he tastes what we call a piece of the "American Pie," he now wants more; he now wants a piece (his piece) of "The American Dream." Then we have all these tough-ass rappers, talking about they're goons, drug lords, shot-callers, have gang-ties and are mob affiliated. But they haven't ever done shit. Instead, they sell and feed this bullshit-ass story to our youths and brainwash them, capitalizing off their vulnerabilities. And through their music, they program them to live in this fairytale movie script which ends in several negative ways:

1. Death

2. Life in Prison

3. Strung out on drugs (starts with the Cush, syrup and mollies).

4. Paralyzed (Trying to be a Goon or Gangbanger)

5. Mentally impaired (due to heavy drug usage)

6. Snitches! (Got caught up trying to indulge in a lifestyle they weren't about and got railroaded and let those folks scare them into flipping on their comrades)

This is what is happening across the globe. These same rappers who are glorifying negativity such as crime, murder, gangbanging and drug abuse, are the same rappers you never heard of until they started rapping. These dudes have no criminal background. These dudes barely copped an ounce of crack, let alone copped a kilogram (1008 grams wrapped up, sealed and stamped). They haven't ever been quoted, blessed or jumped in a gang. They've never been in any drive-byes, gang funerals, gang dorms in the county jail, or under investigation for murder, drugs, or gang validation. But let them tell it, they are the most feared kingpins in their cities. If you pay attention, they're so ass-backwards they wait until they become successful to put up this facade and image. It's all fabricated. There are very few rappers who really live what they rap about and trust me, when I say very few, I mean very few.

This is a topic that a lot of "real" dudes don't want to discuss for fear of being exposed. But this is what's wrong with our brothers and sisters today. We'd rather live in a lie and be happy as persons we're not instead of living in truth and working to become the people God created us to be. We would rather work 40-50 hours a week, slave in fast-food joints and sweatshop warehouses, only to take our check and ball out, buying frivolous merchandise. Why? Just ask yourself, "Do you want to be accepted?" We all want to be praised and viewed as being wealthy, stable, or on top of our game. But the problem is, "**We fake it until we make it.**" Real goons...lol...who're you robbing? How can you be a goon with more bodyguards than the President of the United States (shit even President Obama don't have that many bodyguards), so you got these tough goons walking around with the National Guard. You robbing your own folks. You haven't run into any mansions; you haven't gone down to Hollywood and kidnapped anyone for ransom; and you haven't run up in...Wait. Let me stop. I don't want to give anyone any ideas. My purpose for this book is to drop jewels, right? And to the urban book authors, I respect your work, craft and effort you put into your projects. But a word of advice: think outside of the box.

You can paint pictures of our lifestyle and still deliver <u>real</u>, relevant facts that will inspire the readers. I haven't read an urban book in years. I got tired of the same storylines, kingpins, 1,000 kilos, 1,000 bullets and 1,000 bodies. If you're blessed with a gift to use this pen, rewrite history. Create your own lane. Break the chains of Willie Lynch. Be an asset. Not a liability.

Painted Shackles
By Mr. P. D. White

Incarcerated by my refusal to think outside of the chains that

I've allowed life's experiences to bind and shackle me in;

Suffocated by the pollution that I breathe in when I step

into the air of what many call a community…

In fear of being a victim to my own paranoia-life;

Life to me is L-I-F-E,

Living In Fear Everyday…

Fear of being Michael Brown,

Hands up, shot down.

Fear of being the next Freddie Gray,

Paralyzed, running from death,

"I can't feel my legs."

Fear of being crucified by a racist, atheist as I pray,

in my hometown church 900 miles from Charleston, South

Carolina;

Fear of looking in the mirror and not recognizing the image that

appears.

I am not deaf…I hear the hunger in the stomach of children

who missed another meal because their mothers chose to
feed the monkey on her back; Life is so bananas!

I'm tired of being persecuted; and although I believe Jesus walks
with me, the burden I carry on my back has me asking
Him to please, "Carry this cross with me."

Help! ...SOS…Save Our Souls or Save Our Selves,
or maybe you can just save me from the
embarrassment of failure.

Failing for me is lack of effort. See, I'm encouraged by
the hate of a hater, who hate themselves, so they could never love
me
or understand the love I possess for those close to me.

Your whispers are like fingernails being dug into a chalkboard at a
slow pace.
I hear them; I feel them. Yes, I understand.   You are miserable.
You need company; someone to sit next to you and drink a cup of
"depression" poured from the finest bottle life has to offer.

Sorry, I'm clean and sober: never stressed, always blessed.
I give to you a work of art. My wrist is exhausted.
I will now sit my paintbrush down.

CHAPTER 1

The New Willie Lynch

This is what "Willie Lynch" has done to our communities: "brainwashed" them at the highest degree possible. But a large percentage of our own "folks" are also guilty of doing this to ourselves. As I sit back and listen to what our music has become today, I am convinced that society has become the music and the music has become our society. Music is the new messenger. Music is the new leader. Music is not only influential but it can be held responsible for a majority of the ignorance we see our communities drowned in today. You want to hear something funny? I, too, am a rap artist; "gangsta rap" at that. So I take full responsibility for the role I've played in destroying my own community and the minds of so many innocent youths. That's why I've taken a stand to change the content of my music. The material that's being put out today can be considered somewhat poisonous, with the exception of a few exceptional artists.

For example, take the sister, Nikki Minaj. And just to let you know Nikki, there's no disrespect intended. But she has a large movement, a lot of followers and the majority of them are young enough to be first and second graders. Now when Nikki promotes a song about big butts and shaking your ass for dollars, we all know it'll more than likely climb up the charts and come with an explicit video. But who do you think is sitting in front of the TV screen, mimicking word-for-word and doing all the moves as if they are on the Twister game board? Exactly. Our young girls; our daughters. And don't get me wrong—shout out to Nikki for the real positive, motivational material that she does put out—but some of these kids aren't fully developed mentally to the point where they can separate reality from entertainment. They hear "Barbie" and automatically register the term with the doll in their bedroom. We can't possibly be that naïve and teach our young sisters to "suck dick, get ass shots, get plastic surgery," or "get that nigga for all he got," and not think they are going to just ignore it as entertainment.

It's time that we as leaders and role models perform a self-assessment of what we do, what we say and what we feed into the minds of our youths. God has blessed a lot of entertainers with the talent to speak and deliver our stories in rare form, but we have to remember we have great influence in the same communities which support us and what we promote, and more than likely they will too. To them, we are somebody important; someone they can dream of being. The job you have is a big one but when you signed that contract it is what you signed up for. What sense does it make to get out of the hood but keep your folks mentally confined to the everyday struggles of being in the hood with a ghetto, hood-like mentality? It will not assist them in the real world when they do decide to get a job or enter the corporate world of business. I'm no hater, far from it, and I applaud Nikki and all the other rappers who started from the bottom and built their empires. But also remember that God, or some higher power, put you in that position for a reason. It's your job to figure out what that reason is, not mine. My suggestion is to start teaching our young brothers and sisters' self-respect, integrity and the definition of morals, along with the true power they have to become anything they desire without degrading themselves or the community in which they live.

Another example is Lauren Hill. This sister sold millions of albums and won numerous awards and not once have I ever seen her half-naked and shaking her ass across a stage. She may not have been a sex "icon," but she was naturally beautiful inside and out. She knew that and her objective was to influence women through her self-worth and the empowerment she held. She promoted songs like "That Thang" to preach realness to the sisters and inform them they were worth more than a booty call or a "one night stand." My message to the young sisters—whether black, brown, white, green or yellow—is that respect lends respect. Respect yourself first then others will more than likely respect you also. A man doesn't have to be intimidated to respect you. He just needs to know his place and position. Outer appearance is a major part of the statement "first impressions mean everything," or the ol' sayin', "You never get a second chance to make a first impression." If you were a college graduate, single, a virgin, self-employed and a homeowner out searching for Mr. Right, with the same qualities or better, what kind of man do you think would approach you if you were dressed in high-high heels, ass cheeks hanging out, breasts showing, with a funky-ass jazzy attitude and walk to match your outer appearance? What do you think the average man would assume? Honestly, do you expect to be approached like the true queen you are? For the most part, you should be able to wear whatever it is you choose to wear and still be respected. But the truth of the matter is that's not how many of us brothers operate. Just being 100. And although it's sad to say this, unfortunately, this is the reality of the situation. For us, any sign of easiness is a sign to go in for the kill.

And any type of rebellion is the green light for a man to call you all types of bitches, hoes, tramps and anything else in the ignorant vocabulary that we choose to use to verbally assassinate each other to protect our own image and dignity. Perception is everything, queen. Let me ask you this, would you go to a job interview wearing the type of apparel just described above? No, you would not. Now you're probably rolling your eyes at this book and thinking, "This ain't no damn job interview." You're right, maybe it isn't. But you should also be aware of the fact that you are publicly broadcasting an identity that you truly are not. However, if your profession is that of a stripper, or you work for an escort service, then I guess you are justified in your appearance and the response you receive. However, if you are a hardworking mother, who has self-respect and morals, sister please, put some damn clothes on. When I say clothes, they should not be so damn tight that you get a damn yeast infection when you wear them. Or, think about this, they are so tight that when you eat a Big Mac you are liable to burst out of them!

Always remember this: you never know whom you will run into. You may have a profession that allows you to accidently bump into others in the same job field out in public. Take a RN for instance. The chance of you meeting a doctor with his own practice is rare, but possible. Do you think that your outer appearance matters? I think it does. In fact, I believe it is the difference in him asking you to be a stripper at his bachelor party or asking you to come in for a job interview. Willie Lynch stated "the black (nigger female) with the female offspring will teach her offspring to be like herself, which is independent with a 'what can you do for me' attitude, or the 'something for something' attitude." This is the tactic Willie Lynch taught slave owners to program female slaves with. They also used "phenomena of illusions" to control the female slave. This is something which we see today: money, cars, clothes, handbags, designer-named shoes and the title or status of being the "baddest bitch." This is the "phenomena of illusions" which makes our sisters move.

With the things listed above, you can control a woman's mind, body and eventually her soul. Do you think I am lying to you? Are you the one yelling, "Not me!" Are you sitting there with your face tuned up saying, "I can't be bought." I believe you. I am not out to degrade you or belittle you. But, if a good looking brother pulls up in a Benz, offers to take you shopping, before he takes you out to dinner on the first night, the hard part is done. He has your attention. The values and morals for a percentage of single black women are far below the standards of having good self-esteem. I did not say high self-esteem because having high self-esteem can be dangerous at some point in your life, especially if you become too proud, too arrogant, too conceited and too cocky. God put the queen on earth to be honored and respected. Good self-esteem is a state of mind that says, "I may not be all 'that' but I'm alive, I'm healthy, I'm independent, I'm blessed, I'm living and I refuse to be belittled by anyone or anything." That self assurance lets you know you are someone. Your glow is that of a person who knows they have a lot to be thankful for.

One thing we must all remember is material things can belittle you, especially when you "think" you "need" something to be considered "someone." That thought alone belittles you. When you get your tax return after a hard, long year of work, and as a woman, if the first thing you purchase is a pair of "limited edition" red-bottoms (because you don't want any other chick rocking the same heels you got on), a makeup bag and a new purse, before paying off your credit card bills, catching up on delinquent bills, or paying your rent 4 to 6 months in advance, you have stubbornly and deliberately belittled yourself. You have also belittled your children if you are a single mother. Did you think about investing into their future? Ask yourself this, "Did I make a poor investment?" This is a question you need to ask yourself. "How will I benefit from this investment a year from now?" If your only benefits consist of flashy Instagram photos and hundreds of likes on Facebook, then we got an uphill battle to work on.

However, there is good news. You have taken the first step by purchasing this book. With a poor thought process, we as people tend to pick up bad habits; the same habits we pick up can have a negative effect on our children. In this day and age children are learning much quicker and pick up things much faster. We have to be careful as parents, and even more careful if you are a single mother. What are your values? When you get your taxes, what is the first thing you do when you get your tax check? Did you open up a bank account (savings or CD account)? Did you put some money away for your children's college education? Did you put $500 away for a rainy day? Did you catch up on school shopping? Or, were you like a percentage of those who spent their money recklessly? Balling out. "It's all on me this week," or "I got it homie, don't trip." We must use better judgment when we have access to money. We are taught never to cherish money or value it for more than it's worth as a resource. However, we need to respect it more and not take it for granted. Being broke plays on our mentality in a way that is bad for your health — physically and mentally. My goal in this chapter is to open up the eyes of my young sisters and queens and give them an opportunity to truly get in touch with who they are, their purpose and the power they possess within. Instead of bashing you and telling you what you are doing wrong, I intend on using this opportunity to teach you how to take inventory of yourself and do things better to bring out the best in you and for you. It's time to stop and think about what people value the most.

If you are jobless as you sit and read this book, then believe me what you are about to read and learn in the next chapters will be resourceful and beneficial for your future process. Ask yourself, "what is more important, a job or an image?" I myself am aware of several women who would rather be unemployed than work at a fast-food restaurant. Although I would never encourage anyone to settle for less, slave for minimum wage, or take a pay cut below their qualifications, but I do encourage you to seek employment somewhere. Any job is better than no job at all. It is proven through psychology that a source of income decreases stress in the African American household. There is no feeling like payday. Even if the entire check is applied toward bills, the rent, groceries and transportation it is better than taking a pentenary chance of boosting, engaging in tax scams, selling dope, or even worse, prostitution. The first objective is to become employed. Once you are employed, create a budget. If you receive food stamps, use them wisely which means no excessive eating out. For what? Let's perform some math, even though a lot of us hate math (smile):

- o Let's say you make $300.00 weekly.
- o You have 2 children.
- o You eat out three times a week at McDonald's.
- o You order 2 Happy Meals and 1 adult meal to go for about $15.00 + tax.
- o Now add up that amount for 3 days out of the week.
- o That's $45.00 spent in one week just eating out.
- o Now multiply $45.00 times the 4 weeks in a month. That's $180.00 in fast-food for one month!
- o Now multiply $180.00 times the 12 months in a year. That's $2,160 a year spent on fast-food alone!

Do you know what you can do with $2,160.00? You can invest in a more reliable vehicle; put up money to go back to school; anything but give it away. It is your responsibility as a mother to explain to the kids why they're not eating out this year. Yes, you may receive mean looks, or catch them blowing out air, or even hear cries of "it's not fair," but you are the parent and at the end of the day has to live with the decisions you made. But, there is a solution to their response. Inform your children that instead of eating out, all of you will go grocery shopping for real food—hamburgers, frozen pizza, French fries, chicken wings, gallons of ice cream—and make home cooked meals and have fun night with dinner and DVDs which, may also include popcorn and sodas. These are things that can be purchased at a reasonable price and stored in the refrigerator to be cooked throughout the week. If you receive food stamps, there is an even larger reward for you and the children. Now you can incorporate a steady budget that doesn't include spending unnecessary money for eating out. The objective is to save money and still enjoy the luxury of family life which includes smiles and peacefulness in your household.

LOVE

Love... Think about this word. Ponder on the four letters in this word. What do they mean to you? What is your definition of love? Do you know what real love feels like? If you've read the Bible then you may be familiar with the "love chapter" known as 1Corinthians (1Corinthians 13:4-5)[1] which states, "Love suffers long and is kind; love does not envy; love does not parade itself, it is not puffed up; does not behave rudely; does not seek its own; is not provoked; and thinks no evil." So, ask yourself again, what is *your* definition of love? Has your love life been a painful one? Has your love life been a one-sided lifestyle? Do you constantly feel as if you are putting out more than you are receiving in a relationship? Do you feel as if in order to feel loved you must over-give or put in more than your partner is willing to put in? I've learned from personal experiences that being a loving person comes with its heartaches and pains, especially if you are one that is overly compassionate and is willing to do anything to make your love life work. But one must be careful because sometimes you can love something so much that you begin to see it for what it is and you hate it. That's when the Willie Lynch syndrome takes its toll on your state of mind and you begin to lose the love you once had. At this point you will involuntarily display hate, envy, jealousy; you may even become suicidal or homicidal. For women, it's been labeled by many as the "scorned woman disorder." For men, it's considered the "masculine, dominant, I-refuse-to-be-made-a-fool-of disorder" which is basically pride.

Men have a complex that revolves around competition. This was also a tactic and strategy Willie Lynch mentioned in his famous letter in 1712. "You must pitch the old black male against the young black male, vice versa, also the dark skinned slaves against the light skinned slaves, vice versa." He ends this portion of his speech encouraging slave owners to "pitch the black female slave versus the black male slave, vice versa." If you pay attention to our culture, you can clearly see the separation and segregation. The older black men have no connection with the younger black men. The younger generation is in competition with the older generation. It's as if they want to leave "their mark in the game." The new motto is, "we ain't listening," and the response of the older black males is, "I'm done with them. I've got my own kids to raise."

There is no love. We are living in a ball of confusion. We no longer put our ladies first. Instead, we as men are in competition with the women in our communities. On the one hand you've got "the women empowerment movement," and on the other hand you have the "man's dominance and delusional belief of what his position in a woman's life should be." The woman is yelling, "independent," while the man is dependent on material things in life that reward them with status. Men, we must get our minds out of the gutter. Ladies, it's time to take back your real status as queen and also motivate your men in your life to do better. Sometimes I sit back and ask myself, "Who died and left me in charge?" Seriously. Where did this masochism come from? Where did this "I'm so gangsta, I'm so hood, I got no feelings" and "I'm running shit," come from when in all actuality a lot of us aren't running anything more than our mouths. We are so quick to destroy each other and try to outdo each other that we are blinded by the fact that we are all still very much in the struggle.

Look at what one maniac did in Charleston, South Carolina. He murdered nine beautiful lives, six of which were women.[2] What did you feel? Was it anger? Pain? It must have been an emotion that was indescribable because I know I felt hundreds of different emotions run through my body. The point I'm making is this, if an incident as severe as this can make us as people stop and think about life and how important it is, why can't we do this more often? Why does it take funerals and holidays to bring family together in order to see black people smiling and embracing each other while leaving the negativity outside? And sometimes at functions, even then, we still act as if we are better than each other. We display negative attitudes that can eventually lead us to a local nightclub being shut down, or innocent lives lost behind a small altercation which could have been avoided.

The same negativity that this disturbed kid, Dillon Roof, displayed is the same negativity that many of us display, just on a higher level. He glorifies the Confederate flag, which in many of our eyes is a symbolic mascot for racism. But by the same token, many of our youths are raised and programmed to glorify and fight for flags, or what we call in the community, "Gang Rags," or "Bandanas," which comes in a variety of colors representing different neighborhoods and street organizations. Many of the "flags" or "rags" that our youths die over have generations of bloodshed associated with them. Yet, I don't see many advocates in the black community fighting to change the status of these flags. It's almost become an "if you can't beat 'em, join 'em" attitude. It's as if we pick and choose our battles. We're trying to change things in
America as a whole but we have not even begun to clean up our own backyard. For the young men reading this book, remember that the same colors and rags you represent, they represent years of genocide, hate and prejudice.

Genocide is the number one cause of death in Black America. We don't love ourselves enough to love each other. We don't trust ourselves enough to trust each other. Ol' Willie Lynch preached, "Slaves, they must depend on us, the white race; they must love, respect and trust only us." He was crafty in the way he set the foundation for brainwashing and programming the slave to stay mentally dependent on a higher authority to control and dictate their actions. Willie Lynch informed slave owners that if they did this early, the effects would last a lifetime. Look at us today. It's pitiful, sad, but also true. We are what we believe we are — slaves. Whether it's a slave to violence, material things, money, negative lifestyles, or a slave to our way of thinking, we are still mentally walking around with the slave mentality which our ancestors were programmed to live by. We all scream, "We want a change," but none of us "want to change."

IT STARTS WITH YOU

"He without sin cast the first stone[1]," Jesus stated in John 8:7. In this chapter, a woman was accused of adultery and the people brought her to Jesus and wanted her persecuted and punished under the old laws of Moses which constituted stoning for the act of adultery. Jesus simply told them, in so many words, to go ahead. "If you're guilty of no sin at all, do what you do..." If you know the story you know that no one threw a single stone; not a pebble. Are we pointing the finger? Have you considered taking inventory of your own flaws? When was the last time you looked into a mirror and observed your facial features and just stared at yourself? Try this more often. But don't just stare dumbfounded. Ask yourself, "Who am I?" and, "What changes have I made to make myself a beautiful person inside and out?" "How can I better myself in my current situation?" Ladies and gentlemen, when do we wake up and observe our lives? Are you one of those people who find themselves worried about what is wrong with everybody else? Have you wondered or asked yourself, "Why does he or she get all the rewards in life while I sit here and suffer?" Are you that person in a state of misery and hatred telling yourself, "I deserve to have that, not them?" This is an example of the Willie Lynch slave mentality. We have allowed our programming and circumstances to dictate our lives, minds and how we view others who haven't wronged us.

A lot of our thoughts, views and assumptions are really none of our business. It's time to worry about self, our flaws and inconsistencies; how we can change who we are; and how to become better parents to our children and better children to our parents. It's time to rebuild relationships with our relatives; make amends to friends we've hurt or offended; to put the petty "I'm not calling them first" mentality behind us; and love one another. Life is truly too short to sit around poisoning ourselves with resentment, anger, jealousy and not forgiving. We walk around unhappy and miserable because we worry about everything but the right thing, which is God and ourselves. It's time to be happy again. It's time to live life to the fullest and grasp that feel good attitude. I'm a realist, so I do completely understand that there is so much bullshit that goes on day to day which has an adverse effect on us mentally, emotionally, physically, spiritually, and financially. However, we must not allow these unexpected issues to cause us depression to the point where we hurt ourselves and others.

Unhappy people want nothing more than to make those around them unhappy and miserable. Have you ever met a person with a negative, nasty attitude that changes the energy as soon as they step in the room? A lot of you reading this book are probably shaking your head and have already picked a victim to label as the ruthless villain. How many times have you told yourself, "I'll never be like that person", or "I can't stand that person's attitude." But what happens when you become the villain and the tables are turned? What happens when you stumble or have a bad week and begin to display these same traits? Oh, now you want a little compassion. Now you want everyone around you to understand your current situation and just be a little patient with you. But did you ever stop and consider the other person you judged and persecuted? Did you give them the benefit of the doubt while you sat on lunch break with your employee friends, gossiping and talking about the other person? Did you stop for one minute and ask yourself, "What is this person going through?" Did you offer any type of assistance or encouragement? Did you even approach the "negative" person and ask them, "How is your day?" or "Are you okay?" or "Can I help you with your workload this week?" Or did you just assume they were negative because they enjoyed it?

This is where our people fail. At times I can be so selfish, so self-centered that we lose humanity and humility. We are so quick to judge and so slow to assist. The next time you see a person (sister or brother) going through a phase, try to be patient and humble. Have enough compassion to ask them, "How are you today?" or "How was your morning?" or "How did you feel about that NBA game last night?" or "Did you watch the BET awards?" or "Did you see what such and such had on?" or even, "What you got going on tonight or this weekend? Let's go out and have a drink." A simple act of kindness is all it takes to reverse this sick Willie Lynch theology. As African-Americans we are expected to treat each other like shit. We are programmed to believe that anyone who doesn't "cheerlead" or applaud you for your accomplishments is a "hater." Once you earn the "hater" title, one will stop at nothing to get under your skin and make you hate them even more. This is where the little childish and competitive tactics, to rub it in your face, comes in. At the end of the day the goal now becomes to show you that I'm somebody and you're nobody. This attitude separates the best of friends, family and even relationships. It's time to wake up. We are much better than this. At some point in our lives we must be prepared to either grow together or, grow alone, separated by hate, jealousy, envy and frivolous facades we build in our mind.

The black and Hispanic communities are amongst the most divided in America. We put invisible fences up against our own people. "Keep out." I bet we can't even come up with a logical reason as to why we do this. Maybe I can help explain why. I believe we are mentally manipulated by the enemy who is not your neighbor, your brother at the bus stop, or the sister in the Benz. It's an unseen force of evil which exists wherever you see violence, hate, genocide, drug transaction, prostitution and lost hope. Are you still in the mirror? Are you still ready to pick that stone up and throw it like a major league pitcher? Are you ready to fire it at the person you feel wronged you? Do you have enough realness to take responsibility for your actions, thought processes and the way you've treated others? Are you mature enough to separate the real from the bullshit? Do you have enough love left to not allow the devil to dictate how you deal with others? Is it possible? Yes. But we must be willing to become honest with ourselves, take off the masks and stare at our true identity. We must first look at who we are to understand where we came from and where we're going. For centuries we have lived in a bubble where everything outside of that bubble is foreign to us. It's time to step outside of that bubble, view what's in it and burst it. Let's destroy that bubble which has us mentally shackled and chained. Once we do that, we can smile at the vision we see in the mirror and know deep inside that we've taken the first step at reprogramming our minds.

The Child
By Mr. P. D. White

I'm a man. Shit I got money, cars, clothes hoes and a mouth full of gold.

I'm a man. I let go of my mama's hand when I first came to Uncle Sam's land.

"Home of the killers and school of the hard-knocks" is where I graduated.

My jeans hang lower than my I.Q.; I'm higher than the Rolex I just spent my

Hard-earned blood money on. I stay high and flier than the bullets that soar

in my projects, the same bullets that killed Tameka's son. Damn.

That was my partner. The only one who understood why I never cried…even

when my daddy died. Shit, I just wrapped that bandana around my face and

put black locs over my eyes to conceal the pain.

But I'm a man. I don't need school. I got bills to pay at 13 years old.

So I got a few choices: I can either learn, get smart, get a piece of paper with "Education Earned" on it or I can hustle and get some real paper.

I'm a man. Look at how I roll my blunt and inhale smoke as I change
my son's Pampers and count money all at the same damn time. I hear
it all the time, "You need to grow up; you just don't listen; you're
just like your no good daddy was," all from the same woman who begs,
"Please let me hold a $20 sack till my check come...damn, I'm gone pay you."

So as I put these lil' white crumbs in her lil' dirty black hands and roll my
eyes, I really wanna ask her, "Who's the man now?" All this taking place
while nosey neighbors close their blinds and get on the phone to spread the
gossip like a damn daytime talk show.

"That boy at it again. Won't be long for he dead, just like his daddy, poor boy."
But I shrug my shoulders, put my pistol in my pants, roll my eyes to the world...
I know "I'm a Man."

CHAPTER 2

The New Slave Auction

The new slave auction…"the courtroom"…the new slave plantation: "Prison." Some of the most influential, powerful, smart and wise African Americans are incarcerated. The prison economy is one of the wealthiest marketing corporations around whose revenue largely increases year over year and rarely, if ever, declines. As the crime rates climb nationwide, so does the prison population. The prison corporations make a profit which is seen as a form of extortion when it comes to collect-call phone rates and prison canteen sales. If a prisoner is calling family outside of his prison region he can expect to pay two to three times the normal phone rate for one call. The jobs they provide prisoners are some of the same jobs you can obtain in the free world. The only difference is, in the free world, you are guaranteed what is called minimum wage. In some states this wage ranges from $10.00 to $16.00 per hourly rate for job industries such as janitorial services, clerical, recycle workers, sanitation, HVAC, plumbing, tutoring and data entry. In CDCR (California Department Corrections Rehabilitation) the prisoners who have these same job positions make anywhere from $ .09 to $ .42 per hour, depending upon how long they've held the job. So you must ask yourself, "Where's the other $10.00 - $20.00 prisons are saving hourly to fill these positions? Where does it go?" The average prisoner with a job brings in roughly $45.00 - $50.00 per month.

This money can be used to feed themselves, purchase hygiene products or even send money home to their loved ones. For the prisoners that owe restitution, the state takes an additional 55% out of their initial pay for "victim's restitution." This is nowhere near enough money to feed a grown, hard working man in prison. But they call this "prison" CDCR. If you ask me, I call it modern day slavery. You have a situation where the minority has been placed in a poverty stricken community and the chances of survival are slim to none. Now add in the everyday delusions of having cars, money, clothes and iced-out jewelry to pull the puppet string attached to them and now you have someone who is willing to sell drugs, rob, steal and kill to obtain these prize possessions. The lust causes them to rush into the fast lane to gain wealth which eventually leads to incarceration. Then hold them in the county jail with outrageous bails; raise the prices on canteen; feed them slop infested with mice feces, and it's almost guaranteed they will spend all that hard earned blood, sweat and tears money to survive in the county lockup while fighting the charges against them. The inmate will buy the $ .17 Ramen Noodles at the county jail's ridiculous price of $ .90 to $1.10 per cup of soup. Now leave them in there over a period of time and they will give in to the soup and to the outrageous phone rates of $2.00 - $3.00 per call. By the time they get a half decent attorney, if they can afford one, they'll be broke.

Even worse, if they are sent to prison (the majority are) the system will inform them they must work for the prison they are residing at, or be labeled a "non-complying prisoner who refuses to work." Once this label has been placed in their file, the prisoner will not receive the same privileges as the other working prisoners who are also considered slaves. The privileges for complying with a work order are extra yard time, phone privileges, extra canteen privileges, and a pat on the back from the State. Modern day slavery. It's all a big domino effect system built to profit off the blood, sweat and tears of the prisoners. However, the prisoners can hit them where it hurts without raising one finger — through education.

Every prison has an education department that they will almost force an inmate to enroll in. Recently, CDCR is voluntarily enrolling the young inmates into education straight off the prison bus. But what do most of the young brothers do? They rebel and run from education. If you are a young brother reading this book, and you purposely withdrew from the education department, then I'm addressing you. Most would rather work and slave for CDCR than get an education to better themselves. Let me enlighten you, young brother, O.G. and brother from another. Do you know that right now as I write this book, you got taxpayers and politicians who are pushing to remove education from prison? The way they see it is, "How can a convicted murderer get a free ride through school and he is responsible for the deaths of our children, husbands, wives and friends?" The way they see it is, "We work hard, earn an honest living and can barely afford to send our kids to college. But you can go to prison, get a G.E.D. and get a free college education."

Many of you don't see the bigger picture. It is reported that the State of California spends anywhere from $20,000 - $45,000 to put each prisoner through college. That's tuition, books, computer programs and postage for correspondence courses. But the thing that frequently comes to the minds of the young black male is "Man, they trying to put me in education and make me go to school. Fuck this. I'm trying to get a job in the kitchen and get some extra food," or their homies pump them up with "Oh, I see you in school now. You wasn't in school on the streets." Once again, we are stuck in that old Willie Lynch frame of mind which will hold us back for the rest of our lives if we are not willing to change.

Young brothers and sisters, peep knowledge and wisdom. These jewels I'm about to drop are rare and precious. Regardless of your conviction or current sentence, with education you can exceed much farther in life than without it. I'm sorry, every nickel and dime drug dealer is not fortunate enough to make it to the status of "BIG MEECH" or "FREEWAY RICK ROSS" status. To be honest, the dope game is quite dead but that's an entire other chapter and discussion. If you are currently incarcerated the chances of being the next LeBron James, Marshawn Lynch or Ken Griffey, Jr. is not hopeless, but is getting slimmer each day you spend behind bars. On the other hand, education can be the key to your freedom. The more you know and understand the higher chance you have of getting yourself out of prison. Yes, yourself, pro per. Through reading and writing I've personally witnessed prisoners act as their own attorneys (pro per) and get their cases reversed. It wasn't just the reading and writing that did it, but the understanding of what they were arguing in their appeals (writs) that made a difference. They were able to better articulate their words in the arguments and know the words that they were using. The more you know and learn about the essence of reading the more you can apply it to your reading skills. The more you know about writing, the better you can articulate your words and help the reader get a clear sense of what it is you are writing.

Everyone wants to write an urban book. If that's your dream, go for it. I'll be one of the first people to support you. But if I pick it up and it reads like this: *"He runned to his car cause his leg was brokened cause he get shooted in it and he didn't want to die, but he had to try to run even if he get shot in the leg,"* the first thing I'm going to want to know is who is your editor? Then I'll want to know who wrote this and why. It's not that the script made no sense at all, because as a writer I can pretty much see where you were trying to go, but it was your writing skills which showed me you didn't know how to articulate the words for your reader (who might be a non-writer) to understand you. You don't have to write or spell at a college level to be understood. The average college graduate doesn't write or read at a college level. But you do need to apply yourself with sufficient education in the event you do choose to write an urban novel, poem, rap or even a letter to your loved ones, so that others who read your work will take you serious enough to really read it, appreciate it and respect it. No one wants to read a book full of Ebonics and words they have to figure out.

Then we have this other popular lane that everyone and their mother thinks they belong in: "rapping." Now let's be honest, it's possible for anyone to pick up a mic and tweak their voices, get a beat behind them, perform a rap, put it on YouTube, and become an overnight celebrity. But what happens when it's time to sign that recording contract and you can't even read the damn thing well enough to understand that in no way does the contract benefit you or your career? Let's just say you lawyer-up and pass that stage; easy huh? Now, what happens when you have no math skills past basic arithmetic? How do you manage your money, bank account and your royalties? Even worse, how do you know when your accountant or manager is taking advantage of you? It's time to wake our game up. It's time to do some real soul searching. I'm not telling you to become a genius, a nerd or to square-up. I'm only advising you to wake up. Smell the deception.

A lot of those who read this book are more than likely interested in change of some sort. You may be tired of the lifestyle which landed you in prison, poverty, debt and mental incarceration which have you imprisoned in your own mind. Prison is as close to death that a person can get. It's made to break you physically, mentally, emotionally, spiritually and financially. But think about this: "Try making your negative work as a positive for you." Ask yourself, "How can I make my current circumstances work for me?" If you are in prison as you read this don't let the time do you; do the time and make that time work for you; and make every second on the clock count. Every second you spend incarcerated doing nothing, you are more likely to have that "nothing-ass attitude." It's the same attitude that no one wants to be around once you are released.

Let's take a few minutes and try a small exercise. You will need a pen and some paper. Are you ready? Give yourself a 60 second time limit and write down as many goals as possible that you would like to see yourself achieve in the next five years. This exercise is not just for those incarcerated either. Start now. Are you finished yet? Now take a brief moment and look at the list you just prepared for yourself. Go over each goal you wrote down and start crossing off the ones that you feel are either unrealistic or a longshot. I want you to circle the ones that you feel are achievable. At this point and time in this brief activity I want you to take another sheet of paper and write down the goals that you just circled and leave a couple of spaces in between each one of them. For the next five minutes I want you to look at each goal and after you reach the bottom of the list, sign your name and date it. Take a very deep breath. Inhale...hold for ten seconds...exhale and release.

Now go back and look at each goal. We're going to utilize the space in between each goal for the purpose of explaining how you can achieve each goal and what you intend to do to accomplish these goals. You don't have to write a small story, just a line or two reminding yourself about how you want to go about handling your goals. Here's the catch: you should already have your signature at the bottom of the paper (contract). Now, if you don't attempt to do anything you've listed, you have just lied to yourself. You broke a promise to you. Whether your goal is to quit drinking, stop smoking, stop using drugs, quit gambling, quit cheating, go to church, stop spending money, or to exercise, you should make an honest attempt to complete at least one of your goals within the next two to three weeks. And once you do complete the goal, ask yourself, "How do I feel?" I can almost guarantee you will feel a sense of victory.

After doing this exercise and successfully completing a goal or two, treat yourself to a small reward such as a nice meal, pray a quick prayer thanking the god you serve, or go online and inform the world of your accomplishments and challenge others to do the same thing.   You can do this with encouraging words informing them that it was hard in the beginning but if you can do it they can do it. This is a positive start at rebuilding you. There is a war and it's not just against the black race, it's against the entire human race. Those with political power and influence over the world cannot properly carry out their responsibilities unless we as humans are factored into them, too. A lot of our every day stress, fears and anxiety comes from things that are totally out of our control. Gas prices are at an all-time high. I chose this topic to show you just how much control politics and the economy plays in our lives. Every time the gas prices go up, how does it make you feel? Now think about that question for a minute because no matter how wealthy you are this does eventually affect you and your finances.

Let's break down a scenario. For the past 60 days your attitude has been fairly balanced and moderate. Then you got up on Monday morning, performed your normal routine which was to pray, shower, get dressed and get your son up and ready for school. Looking at the clock you realize you are pressed for time, so you and your son exit the house, get in the car and prepare to start your day on a good note. As you sit in the car you look into the rearview mirror, smile at your son who is a 12-year old young man with a promising future in basketball. You turn up your music, probably a little Beyoncé or Jill Scott, and you bob your head.

Today is a good day. As you leave your community, you smile and wave at the other neighbors who are also starting their daily routines. When you pull to the stop sign you realize that your gas tank is almost on empty. You figure this is the perfect time to fill up your tank and grab your son a few snacks before dropping him off to school and heading to work. As you pull up to the gas station, your facial expression changes as if you were a werewolf in a Stephen King movie. "Oh, hell naw!" you mumble. It seems as if overnight the gas prices have skyrocketed from $2.79 a gallon to $3.70 a gallon, and you have a small SUV which means it takes a little bit more than average to fill up your tank.

You begin to drive over to the gas pump area as you do the mental math in your head, but you are interrupted. "Mom, can you get me one of those Lunchables with the cookies in it this time? Remember, you promised me."   Not even realizing your frustration, you turn around and begin to scream at your son about always asking for something and how he gets on your damn nerves, and how you wished his sorry-ass daddy wasn't in prison...STOP. Do you see the control you lost over this situation which you never had control over? Do you see how you allowed your emotions to run rampant? This is a real life scenario that goes on in the lives of many young kids and their parents. For some, this is normal. How do you think a young man feels when you say these hurtful things to him? Mothers, if every time you are faced with minor adversities, or even major setbacks and you lash out, blaming the child and his father for your problems, you have poisoned him with the Willie Lynch syndrome. You have followed proper protocol for the Willie Lynch philosophy and turned son against father, young against old.

You can believe that the rage in the young boy is growing so strong that he may go to school angry enough to act out in a violent manner. Now the domino effect starts. Take notice to what I am now presenting to you. Your son arrives at school with no Lunchables, feeling hurt and a kid he already isn't fond of just so happens to say the wrong thing to him. Your son punches the kid and ends up getting suspended. When the principal informs you of his actions you still continue to blame your son, bash his father and insult your son by calling him dumb or saying things like, "You're going to end up just like your dad." You never considered your reaction to an action that caused an adverse negative reaction from him. Then you have the nerve to ask him, "What the hell is wrong with you?" You can predict that his answer will be, "I don't know," because he doesn't. He's too young to understand the effects of his mother's negative outburst and how it had an effect on his mood and attitude.

Now, let's entertain a deeper picture of this scenario. The young man is 12 years old, suspended for a week, and you have no one to watch him because you must go to work; you can't afford any days off. The first thing you say when you get home is, "You can't lay around here all day eating up shit, running up the bills while I work. So when I leave in the morning you gotta leave, too. I don't care what you do." The average 12-year old boy from a poverty-stricken community or the projects may jump for joy. But remember, this is a young man who does fairly good in school and enjoys playing basketball. He's really not too happy himself about the suspension. Young males usually have two or more older friends that they look up to. I know I did. These kids they look up to may not be in school and may be involved in things that we as parents try to keep our kids away from. With the actions you just read about, you can bet you will push your child right into the hands of those who will more than likely influence him to get into trouble. The mother in the scenario has opened a door that she is not prepared to deal with. Is this you? Have you been the parent who stubbornly lashed out at your kids for reasons which were unexplainable? These unpredictable outbursts and hurtful ways of dealing with our children can become the reasons they turn to gangs, drug use, drug dealing, robbery and a long list of horrible things which will haunt you and the child for a long time. Once the child feels abandoned you can bet they will find more interest in the things listed above than they will in school.

As I write this book I reflect on my youth. I was the 12-year old child that I just mentioned. The gas station scene never took place, but I experienced everything else I mentioned. When life was hard on my mother she was hard on me and my younger brother. I was the oldest. The weight of the world was placed on my shoulders at a young age. I would go to school with that stress, frustration and anger which caused me to act out. My mother was a young, single parent, raising three kids on her own with little to no help from our fathers. It was two boys and one girl. Although my mother was employed, it was barely bringing in enough to maintain bills, clothe and feed us. My mother often told me stories about how, after I was born, she got put out the house. We had to live in abandoned houses, climbing through windows, trying to escape the cold winter nights, only to be discovered the next day by the landlords and asked to leave. She said she even pleaded a few times, "Please just let us stay here until the next day," but was always told no. This would place any single, first-time mother in a messed up state-of-mind. From experience I've learned that situations like this can either make you or break you.

Moving on through life we experienced living in trailer parks. These trailers were no joke! Upgrading to the projects was even worse. It wasn't even the situation or circumstances that we were in that frustrated me as a child. It was those statements she would make about "the bills and my father." This placed me in a difficult position as a young man. I was a straight "A" student in school, played every sport and was a talented rapper. You could say I had somewhat of a promising future. But my mother's situation pushed me into a life of selling drugs, breaking into homes and eventually drug and alcohol abuse at 12 years of age. I don't blame her. How can I? You put any single mother in a stressful situation and if she is not equipped with the proper life skills to survive, she will eventually break under the pressure. With all the circumstances and cards stacked against the young black female, if she is surrounded by drugs, poverty and negativity, it's more than likely she will indulge in drug use or some form of get-away: excessive partying, drinking, or even unusual sexual activity that consists of multiple sex partners.

Through life experiences and dealing with a number of women in different races, I found out that this is just not a problem in the black urban community; this is a problem everywhere. It doesn't matter if the single mother is black, white, Asian, Hispanic or another race. If they have no moral family support, proper job training skills and little to no help from the father of the children she provides for, there is a chance that she will fall victim to the negative vices of society. They may turn to cigarettes to calm their nerves, drinking to drown their misery away and other drugs (such as weed) to give them that relaxed state-of-mind; even crack and powdered cocaine to give them that quick release. It has become mental warfare. When the drug of their choice no longer reaches the tolerance level of "high," they eventually tend to turn to another drug to seek that feeling of "high" they can no longer achieve with a drug of lesser potency. In the hood you have your choice of drugs: coke, pills (mollies), cush (weed), painkillers (methadone, oxycotins), syrup (promethizine, hydrocodone), and other things that a young, lost mother can find false hope in.

The New Willie Lynch   Concrete Walls & Steel Bars
Mr. P. D. White

Now just imagine that 12-year old boy we discussed earlier no longer walking in his own footsteps to become a productive factor in his household. He is now tracing the footsteps of his father, and his father's father. A free ride to prison. This is the leverage that lawmakers and politicians use to incite fear into taxpayers to push for harsher laws and harsher prison sentences. These laws are created and directed toward the young black and Hispanic men and women (See table sentenced prisoners). If they can remove the first half of this story, and sell the public the second half, they can convince taxpayers and voters that our youth are a threat to society and the American dream. They paint a majority of young black and Hispanic males as gang members. This is a typical stereotype they place on any male of color who dresses in what they call "thug apparel." With animated movie-like scripts, politicians make taxpayers believe that these same young men display violent characteristics and if given the opportunity they will eventually victimize you. Once this story is sold to the public, taxpayers will feel more comfortable paying taxes to fund the building of new prisons and more law enforcement officers. Therefore, when new bills are brought to the table for harsher prison sentences such as the death penalty and three strike laws, the traumatized story buyers will support the new laws.

Now you have normal American citizens going out and arming themselves with firearms in fear of becoming prey to those "predators" who lurk the streets that they have been warned about. The government uses reverse psychology to obtain their agenda and goals. This is only my opinion. But what else is the public supposed to think when you sell a storyline such as, "these young thugs are menaces to society; they are predators who prey on the weak. They will rob, steal and kill you…but for a small fee we will uphold the law and protect you from those savages. We will keep them in fenced-in communities (projects), we will not allow them to leave set perimeters (ghetto), and their drugs and violence will not reach you (suburbs)." Then the icing is put on the cake when you have the media as the major instigators by labeling every suspect as an "ex-con/ex-felon," or "parolee," or "convicted felon" who committed a heinous crime. So when it's time to bring new bills to pass to become new laws, you not only have the full attention of the taxpayers and wealthy citizens with political influence, but you also have their support. These people can be labeled "the prey."

One thing humans refuse to embrace is fear, or something they don't understand. We rebel against it. We run from it. We don't even have to experience being hurt by someone or something to fear it. It's a human instinct to fear. If we perceive danger or something as a threat, that alone is enough to put us in a traumatic state of mind when confronted with our fears. Ask yourself, "Have I ever been attacked by a vicious St. Bernard (large dog) with rabies?" The answer is probably no! However, if you've seen the movie "Cujo" by Stephen King, you are more than likely to vividly remember the terror the animal caused the young child and his mother. And even though a St. Bernard is nowhere near as vicious as the movie portray them to be, you will assume every large dog is aggressive and will attack you. The same thing happens with humans on an everyday basis. We assume if a few bad apples make bad decisions and we can associate them with a specific class or group of individuals, then all of them are the same. Do you see where I'm going with this? "Prisoners," the "bad group of people," who made the same mistakes most of us made growing up. Why is it that every time a young black or Hispanic male is shot down by law enforcement the first thing the media reports is, "officer shoots unarmed man who is a parolee or convicted felon," and then they spotlight they portray the victim's background history as a life of crime and bad character.

We as a whole must change. It's going to have to start with you and your willingness to change your attitude and way of thinking in order to find peace, especially if you have children. Let me share some true facts and data with you that you may or may not be familiar with. This data consists of the number of prisoners incarcerated in 2013, by race, gender and age. The statistics also break the numbers down state by state. I will use this data to show you how the states with the most prisoners of color are also some of the states with the highest poverty rates. I will also provide you with a clear picture of how these same cities in these states are labeled some of the most violent cities in America, and how these are the same cities and states that have made national headlines for police brutality and police shootings:

●Between 2012 and 2013, male prisoners increased 0.2% (2,500) similar to 2012; non-Hispanic blacks (37%) comprised the largest portion of male inmates under state or federal jurisdiction in 2013 compared to non-Hispanic whites (32%) and Hispanics (22%).

●White females comprised 49% of the prison population compared to 22% black females. However, the imprisonment rate for black females (113 per 100,000) was twice the rate of white females (51 per 100,000)[1].

●Almost 3% of black male U.S. residents of all ages were imprisoned on December 31, 2013 (2,805 inmates per 100,000 black male U.S. residents) compared to 1% of Hispanic males (1,134 per 100,000) and of 0.5% of white males (466 per 100,000) (See table).

●While there were fewer black females in state or federal prisons at yearend 2013 than in 2012, black females were imprisoned at more than twice the rate of white females.

●For males ages 18 to 19—the age range with the greatest difference in imprisonment rates between whites and blacks— black males (1,092 inmates per 100,000 were black males) were more than nine times more likely to be imprisoned than white males (115 inmates per 100,000 were white males).

•The difference between black and white female inmates of the same age was smaller but still substantial. Black females ages 18 to 19 (33 inmates per 100,000) were almost five times more likely to be imprisoned than white females (7 inmates per 100,000)[2].

•Equivalent proportions of black (58%) and Hispanic (60%) prisoners were convicted of violent crimes (offenses), while the percentage of white inmates (49%) serving time for violent crimes were smaller[3].

This information is available online when you Google the sources provided in the Footnotes section of this book. What this data is showing us is that we, as a minority, are losing a majority of our young brothers and sisters to modern day slavery through these prison slave plantations. Just imagine if a majority of these individuals were given a real opportunity to be productive in society. There would be no limitations on the goals that could be achieved when we are talking about rebuilding the communities we live in. Most of the prisoners in these surveys may not have the education equivalent to that of a third grade student. Another portion of them dropped out of school because of the same circumstances discussed earlier in the chapter. There were other factors that played a role in the crimes they committed other than just gangs and drugs. You have fatherless households, others were raised by foster parents, and some were orphans and never experienced having parents. So when we look at the percentage of black and Hispanic males and females who are incarcerated, you may want to read deeper into those numbers and ask yourself, "What was going on in the homes of these individuals which made it a common, everyday thing for these young black men and women to become victims of society and throw their lives away behind bars?"

In the next chapter we will discuss some of the mitigating factors that many face on a day-to-day basis. Have you ever heard of the expression, "to each one teach one?" This is what we are missing nowadays. The reason is simple. A majority of our fathers, leaders and role models are either dead or in prison. The dominant males who had a voice are locked away, leaving the young black men to fight for themselves; leaving the next generation to groom and mold themselves. While growing up, I was fortunate enough to have a few older cats to lace me up and show me how to be a real man, even though I still chose to participate in the street hustle. They taught me the importance of education. This type of mentoring is no longer available. A lot of those O.G's have moved on, died, or become prisoners. By the numbers, here are the 20 most dangerous cities in America:

Posted May 8, 2015, by Tribune Media Wire:

1.   Detroit, MI
2.   Oakland, CA
3.   Flint, MI
4.   Memphis, TN

5.   St. Louis, MO
6.   Cleveland, OH
7.   Little Rock, AR
8.   Baltimore, MD
9.   Milwaukee, WI
10.   Rockford, IL
11.   Birmingham, AL
12.   Atlanta, GA
13.   Washington, D.C.
14.   Kansas City, MO
15.   Newark, NJ
16.   Indianapolis, IN
17.   New Haven, CT
18.   Buffalo, NY
19.   Stockton, CA
20.   Miami, FL

- With Detroit leading in violent crimes, including murder, rape, robbery and aggravated assault, it's no wonder why this city is the poorest city in America and remains poverty-stricken with no solution to date.

- Number 2 was Oakland, California. We all remember the murder of unarmed Oscar Grant who was gunned down by transit police. The city witnessed a police chief who resigned and multiple investigations into the "riders" which were later revealed to be a secret "gang" inside the Oakland Police Department. They participated in multiple crimes such as extortion, police brutality, coerced confessions, drug transactions, suspicious deaths and a list of other crimes which are still being investigated. A lawsuit was brought against the city of Oakland, who is still paying the victims of harsh police brutality.

- Number 5 was St. Louis which was at the center of attention the entire year of 2014 and 2015 for the senseless death of Michael Brown in the neighboring town of Ferguson. His death sparked riots, a spike in crime and an investigation into racial profiling which was being used by the police department in both Ferguson and St. Louis.

- Number 6 was Cleveland, Ohio which was the center of attention for one of the most hideous police shootings bar none. Two unarmed black citizens, one male and one female, were shot to death after their car backfired and the officer claims he assumed they were firing a firearm at him and other officers. There was a reported 137 empty shell casings found at the crime scene. The car was literally shredded into scrap metal.

- Last, but not least, is number 8 Baltimore, Maryland. This city was put on blast by not only the media and citizens, but also the mayor expressed her disgust for the police force and how they handled Mr. Freddie Gray's arrest in what some believe was a murder. This sparked riots, businesses were burned down, police cars were vandalized and retaliation by law enforcement, who were the original perpetrators that caused the whole scenario.

Out of the top 20 most dangerous cities in America, there are multiple stories for each city which include poverty, crime, police brutality and other senseless scenarios. What I wanted to do was provide you, the reader, with a clear picture of how these same cities have some of the most historical issues in the news right now pertaining our youth.

Prisoners Under State or Federal Jurisdiction, by Gender, December, 2013

Jurisdiction Total Male Female

Jurisdiction	Total	Male	Female
California	135,981	129,684	6,297
Maryland	21,335	20,410	925
Michigan	43,759	41,700	2,059
Missouri	31,537	28,755	2,782
Ohio	51,729	47,579	4,150

When looking at these results provided by the National Prisoner Statistics Program you must remember that California is the larger of the five states listed although, the prisoner rates are still staggering in other states which have smaller populations but are more poverty stricken communities than the average American state, city or town. Over the next few pages I will provide you with the crime rates and the populations of those five cities I mentioned earlier.

- In 2013, the population of Detroit was listed at 706,663. The violent crime rate was 2,052.5 crimes per 100k people:

Murders - 316
Rape   - 618
Robbery - 4,774
Assault - 8,796
Total of **14,504** violent crimes

• In 2013, the population of Oakland was listed at 397,011. The violent crime rate was 2,011 crimes per 100k people:

Assault - 2,792
Robbery - 4,922
Rape   - 180
Murder   -   90
Total of **7,984** violent crimes

• In 2013, the population of St. Louis was listed at 318,955. The violent crime rate was 1,591.8 crimes per 100k people:

Assault - 3,167
Robbery - 1,457
Rape   - 333
Murder   - 120
Total of **5,077** violent crimes

• In 2013, the population of Cleveland was listed at 394,335. The violent crime rate was 1,458.4 crimes per 100k people:

Assault - 1,789
Robbery - 3,490
Rape   - 417
Murder   -   55
Total of **5,751** violent crimes

- In 2013, the population of Baltimore was listed at 621,445. The violent crime rate was 1,404 crimes per 100k people:

  Assault - 4,460

  Robbery - 3,734

  Rape   -   298

  Murder -   233

Total of **8,725** violent crimes

Those were the circumstances many of these young brothers and sisters find themselves in; products of their environments. Our communities and surroundings often stereotype us as thugs and drug dealers who are responsible for the large crime rate numbers in such small cities and towns. The cities that many expected to make the list of 20 didn't. We could easily assume cities such as Houston, Chicago, New York City, Los Angeles and New Orleans would have made the list but they didn't, and it wasn't simply due to the population standards because many of those cities have serious crime issues. It was due more to the fact that the cities listed were some of the most poverty stricken cities. Also, the employment rate was below average, the dropout rate for kids was steadily climbing and prison rates were increasing, leaving children to raise themselves in what was already a negative uphill battle.

Faith
By Mr. P. D. White

Here I sit in a chair I had faith would not break and cave in as I sit down on it.

Is it odd? I had more faith that the chair would hold me and stop my fall,

but I don't even show that same faith in the God I call.

Is it safe to say I am misled by my own belief of what faith is?

I once told a woman, "How can you be faithful to me when you're not even

faithful to God?" That discussion was the discussion that now has us at odds.

I put more faith into the belief this gun won't jam up than I have in my God,

preventing me from being shot.

Faith? I got more faith in my "friends' avenging my death

than I have in being protected by a cop.

Where I'm from its cop and blow, cop some dope;

My faith is in the weed, calming my nerves therefore,

my belief is I gots to smoke.

This Newport 100…I am 100, but only show 99.9% love to my kids

who have faith that Daddy loves them more than cars, clothes and money.

Instead I kept it "1 thousand" with my block and avoided responsibility of

fatherhood like I avoid bullets with my name on 'em and duck shots.

Pac once said, "Who do you believe in?"

Well…as I sit down, I guess it's this chair that has yet

to crumble beneath me…

CHAPTER 3

What's Really Going On?

"Brother, brother, there're far too many of you dying"
Marvin Gaye, "What's Goin' On"

Data gathered from The National Center for Fathering (http://www.fathers.com/statistics-and-research/the consequences of fatherlessness) inform us that children from fatherless homes are more likely to be poor, become involved in drug and alcohol abuse, drop out of school and suffer from health and emotional problems. Boys are more likely to become involved in crime and girls are more likely to become pregnant as teens. Children in father-absent homes are almost four times more likely to be poor.[1] Children living in households headed by females with no spouse present had a poverty rate of 47.6%, over four times the rate in married-couple families.[2] "There is significantly more drug use among children who do not live with their mother and father."[3]

In African-American communities, you can almost walk through and sense a different energy as soon as you enter them. You have those who are depressed, angry, and frustrated. Then there are those who are happy. In my household it wasn't rare to smell weed or find joint roaches in the ashtray. There were times

90

where I opened the refrigerator and there were bottles of beer; easy for me to access. Had I been warned about the danger behind drugs and alcohol at an early age, I may have steered in a different direction. Sure, my mother would scold me and tell me not to bother her stuff, and of course we had drug and alcohol awareness at school. But when you are surrounded by drug and alcohol use and it seems as if this is what everyone around you are doing (even the parents), then its kind of hard for a child to walk away from something so tempting which seems to make everyone else around him happy. Can you imagine growing up in a community where you witness your friends you've known since childhood die in a violent shootout, or an innocent bullet that wasn't meant for them? Can you fathom the reality of walking into your mother's bedroom to show her your report card and you catch her with a large glass pipe in her mouth, or you see a mound of white powder on her Rihanna CD case with a straw next to it? Can you stomach the thought of not having a father around to teach you how to play sports, fight or ride a bike, and every time you talk to him he has an excuse for not coming to see you or he makes another broken promise? These are real life scenarios for our inner city youths. And the nation wonders why everyone is running around high on any drug they can find. It's because they are hurting. It's not a physical pain but more of an emotional and mental pain that can drive a young child to commit suicide if they aren't mentally strong enough. "Children of single parent homes are more than twice as likely to commit suicide."[4]

When you look at these facts, you must also look at the circumstances and realize that this is happening in some of our households, right next door or down the street. It's almost impossible to turn a blind eye when you look at things from the outside looking in, but what happens when you are on the inside looking out? For some of you it may be hard to read this book and deal with the fact that your child could be a part of the percentage that actually carryout their thoughts of suicide. Sometimes the answers are right in our faces and we ignore them because we are too busy to take a few hours out of our busy schedules to attend to the needs of our children.

While we are online searching for the next pair of exclusive pumps, or on Facebook, Twitter and Instagram, our children are suffering from a lack of love, understanding attention and commitment on our behalf. True enough, the presence of both parents is statistically important. However, does that give us an excuse for not going "hard in the paint," chin up and chest out, seeing to it that our children know they are loved. We just lost the daughter of the late, great Whitney Houston — Bobbi Kristina. That is an example of a child dying of thirst from lack of guidance from the two people who were supposed to protect her: her mother and father. IF WE THINK WE ARE READY FOR CHANGE WE MUST BE READY TO CHANGE!!

It's our duty as parents to be better role models for our children. They didn't ask to come here (into the world) so while they're here let's show them they are loved, adored, cared for and needed. It's our duty to educate our children about the dangers and consequences of drug and alcohol use. We must teach them about the do's and don'ts when it comes to the streets and the influences of their peers. We must be willing to listen to them and not be judgmental as if we never made mistakes. If you listen to them, a kid will tell you everything you want to know. Sometimes you must come down to their level, even if that means playing John Madden 2015 with your son. Whatever you need to do to make him open up, do it. You must live with the outcome of that child's life.

Study data shows that children born to single mothers show higher levels of aggressive behavior than children born to married mothers[5], and may be due to the absence of a dominant male authority in the household. From experience I've personally observed mothers who are a little more lenient with children when they are younger. However, by the time the children become older, they are so used to getting their own way that anything else will cause them to rebel. This only points out how very important it is to discipline our kids at an early age and set ground rules. You may have to become both mommy and daddy. The rewards outweigh the struggle.

Fathers it's time for us to do our jobs, period. There are no excuses acceptable when it comes to the precious lives of our children. It's proven that 71% of high school dropouts are fatherless. Fatherless children have more trouble academically; they score poorly on tests of reading, mathematics and thinking skills; children from father-absent homes are more likely to be truant from school; more likely to be excluded from school; and more likely to leave school by 16 years of age.[6] This alone proves that the male presence in the child's life is more than important no matter how we look *at* it. We find ourselves in certain situations because we choose to ignore our true responsibilities until it's too late. It seems when a brother finds himself behind bars, all of a sudden his children become the apple of his eye; the most important thing God has put into his life. But, when he was free, he rarely spent any time with them. If he did, it was brief hi and bye. He might purchase a pack of Pampers and come through with a few dollars for the mother of his child, but he really played no role in the upbringing of his child.

Brother, if you think for one minute you can escape your responsibility you are only fooling yourself. If you don't raise them someone else will. More than likely they will turn to a life of crime. "Adolescents living in intact families are less likely to engage in delinquency than their peers living in non-intact families. Compared to peers in intact families, adolescents in single-parent families and step-families were more likely to engage in delinquency."[7] The dropout rate for black ninth graders is 4.3%, for Hispanics 3.5% and whites 2.1%. The race/ethnicity distribution of the population from which these dropout rates were calculated is 13.7% black, 22.3% Hispanic and 51.9% whites.

For the brothers that are incarcerated and reading this book, you can still make a change and become a role player in the life of your children. Just a simple letter to start a new bridge of communication is all it takes to get the ball rolling. If you have a means of contacting the mother of your children, and the two of you don't see eye-to-eye, remove all selfish motives and remember this is not about you and her, but about the children the two of you still have a duty to raise. If the kids are old enough to read then write nice little letters, speaking in their language and let them know daddy loves them. Draw pictures for them and if you can't draw make an attempt to find someone who can. Every little girl and boy likes a cartoon character on a card from their daddy. The purpose is to begin being involved in their lives. This is a point in your life where you can do something positive and productive for all the right reasons — your kids.

You set the tone as a man. If you are successful and involved in your child's life, it is important your child know they are important in your life. You must value your kids just as much as you value your cars, rims, girlfriends, designer clothes and your homies in the hood. Many of us will go out of our way to stick to the G-code and stand up for the hood and the homies in the hood, but won't even put forth half of this effort for the children we are responsible for. Right now there is some brother locked away for his "homies" who haven't sent him a dime, not to mention buying his kid a Pamper or birthday gift. But that's who we show our love and loyalty to. You've got a lot to learn young man. It's cool to have love for your boys, but your kids come first!

When our sons and daughters reach the age of understanding and begin to question the whereabouts of their fathers and mothers, we are responsible for supplying them with answers. What do you tell a 15-year old young man who has experienced the effects of not having a male role model in his household? One who has been severely influenced by the society he lives in which may consist of gangs, drugs, prostitution and other negative influences. What response do you give him when he asks the question, "Where was my father and why wasn't he around to protect me?" From a daughter's perspective, depending upon the life-changing experiences she has gone through, this can have an adverse effect which may cause her to question the whereabouts of the father and eventually turn to another authoritative male figure for guidance and direction. What do you tell your daughter who has just turned 14 and has been a victim to rape? What answer do you provide her as to why you were absent in her life? How do you try to be a father—after 15 years—to a young man who is now a gang member, drug user and convicted felon? These are the questions some of America's African-

American fathers need to ask themselves, now, before their children reach these ages and experience these unfortunate events. If you are a father with small kids, and you have not been a factor in their lives, now is a good time to start; better late than never.

When I first lived with my father, I had just turned 17 years old. I'd been exposed to the lifestyle of the projects way of living which consisted of gangs, drugs, violence and other negative influences. I was a drug user who had already experimented with weed, alcohol, smoking sherm sticks and sniffing powdered cocaine. I had also been to several funerals of my homies who had passed away. Even though my father had a career, lived a steady lifestyle and tried to compensate for the loss of time, it was evident that it was far too late for him to try to father me and mold me into the young man I should have been molded into at an earlier age in life. I'm at a wise stage in my life where I hold no grudge or point the finger at him. But how many young men and women actually reach this level of forgiveness and understanding? I believe for me to become a father I had to go to jail, miss a substantial amount of time from my kids' lives and watch them grow up from inside a prison cell. It took all of this for me to realize that things do happen and not every parent purposely avoids responsibility. I, too, would want my children to understand my situation and forgive me, so that allowed me to have understanding and forgive my father.

The Willie Lynch teaching and programming was structured to keep the child and parent at odds with each other, especially the young male and the older male. This is one of the greatest reasons many kids grow up not forgiving their parents for being absent in their lives. This is an important factor which every household should consider when raising children. It is time to sit down and ask ourselves, "How can I do better?" How can we become better mothers, fathers, grandparents and relatives if we are not willing to first work on ourselves so that we are better assets to our families and communities?

Let's take a brief moment and go back a few steps to the last chapter where I discussed the gas station scenario. As you bob your head to the music playing through your speakers, you pull up to the gas station. "Are you serious?" you mumble as you realize the gas price has skyrocketed overnight. Instead of allowing this minor inconvenience to ruin your day, take a deep breath; a long one if needed. If you are spiritual, you may want to consider saying a quick prayer to brush off any unnecessary evil or negative thoughts that may be ready to penetrate your mind. Inhale...exhale...smile. Recent studies in psychology insist that smiling, especially during stressful events, can alter the mind into calming down. It is said to be effective due to our mind's ability to relate smiling with a pleasant moment or emotion. If you want to test this theory, don't think just start smiling right now for the next 15 - 20 seconds. How do you feel? Did it work for you? If it did you may want to consider practicing this more often when you find yourself in a stressful situation.

Now as you sit in that car, hands on the steering wheel, look in your rearview mirror and look at your precious, innocent, handsome son in the back seat and smile. Negative energy is easy to feel and sense so try giving off positive energy, especially to a child. As your son pops that question, "Mom, can I get a Lunchables?" Instead of lashing out, say something more along the lines of, "Baby, they've raised the gas prices again. I may not have enough today. You may have to eat at school. We'll see. No matter what, I'll be sure to make it up to you once I get paid this week." And to top it off, end your statement with a big, "I love you," and a smile. I can almost promise you the results will be much different than before. If you go into the store, pay for gas and if you have a little loose change leftover, try grabbing him a small snack just to show you made an effort to hold true to your promise as his mother. And if his father is incarcerated, try convincing or encouraging your son to write him before you hand the snack to him. You may want to even throw it out there like, "When was the last time you wrote your father?" Don't say, "When was the last time you wrote your sorry-ass daddy?" Not only will it hurt the child's feelings if he looks up to his father, but if he already holds some type of resentment or grudge against him, more than likely, he will not be eager to write his father. And when you arrive at his school and drop him off, try telling him,

"Have a good day, stay out of trouble" and "I love you." Saying things of that sort will encourage him to make you proud of him. You may want to think of something fun that the two of you can do at the end of the week once you do get paid.

My intentions are to reach the reader with real life scenarios that could happen to any one of us at any given time. My purpose is to give you a sample of how our responses to our children can be the difference in them becoming one of the statistics in a data survey, or moving through life being productive individuals who don't allow their circumstances to keep them stagnated in neutral. It begins with working on self and having self-discipline when it comes to attitudes, language use and activities we participate in within the presence of our children. Learn how to be slow to anger, slow to speak and quick to hear. Sometimes it's best to digest and take in what is being said and pause. Don't even respond. First, allow your brain to register what you are hearing. Then ask yourself, "Is the feeling I'm feeling altered?" "Do I really feel like this?" Or you may even question yourself and ask, "Did this particular person, place, or thing put me in this state of mind?" If your answer is consistent with your thought process being altered, then you may want to change it, quickly!

If you remember, I mentioned my mother's situation and how she found herself responding to a lot of things I did as a child which also contributed to how I viewed things, took things in and responded to stressful circumstances. As children, we grow up with a lot of unrealistic goals and hopes. One of my goals was to make my mother happy at any cost, no matter what it took. When she complained about money and bills and would lash out about the role my father should be playing, this pushed me to do what I felt was my part—as a young man—to help around the house more and take the load off her back. In my young mind, selling drugs, committing burglaries and stealing was the easiest way to bring money in to help my mother pay bills which seemed to stack up. I must admit, I was good at what I did; so good that my negative lifestyle had a positive impact in the household. My younger siblings were fed, a few bills were paid and my mother was happy. This gave me the feeling of being a MAN! I hustled and I took in everything that came with the hustle, including using the type of drugs I described earlier in the book which later included ecstasy, and syrup. I began to carry concealed weapons, run with a much older, established group of people and picked up some bad habits which were truly not in my character of being a smart young man who enjoyed playing sports, performing music and brought home A's and B's consistently, year after year. It was almost as if at the age of 12 I transformed into something I wasn't born to be: a menace.

After being suspended from school a lot I began to get expelled year after year and eventually started attending alternative schools. I ended up in a group home, passed through the juvenile system's "hall phase" to finally living in a prison cell. It wasn't until 2007, after I was arrested in California, that I woke up. It took experiencing the good ol' California justice system to realize there wasn't justice at all. And if that was what it looked like then I needed to see an eye doctor because it was the blurriest picture I'd seen in a long time since being born into this world in 1980. I see why the lady who is supposed to represent the justice system wears a blindfold. She doesn't even want to see this corrupt system which has gotten out of hand. I think we can thank Willie Lynch for his contributions to the most influential teachings that are still in effect to this day. He deserves the credit. I've been hoodwinked!

A Baby Bird

By Mr. P. D. White

Falling. That's what we all do when we come down off of that high.

Rather it had me on my high horse or soaring like an endangered species.

I must admit, I was in the sky and it felt good until I crashed.

At last my body splashed against the earth, in touch with the reality of the

Fact that I'm no different than this dirt…the same dirt I've fallen in.

Well, at least that's how I feel. My high is gone; no more wings, sober and still…

"Chirp-chirp-chirp," the sound awakens me from my grief,

As I quickly turn and notice the sound that comes from under the leaf…

that I'm next to. My best move would be to ignore the sound, that has consumed my attention as I lay on the ground.

But curiosity finds me and I'm lost for words,

as I turn over this leaf and see a Baby Bird.

"Oh little fella, it seems as if you've fallen, too,

it seems as if you've also allowed the cruels

of this world to discombobulate you."

Was it your stubborn neglect of the warning chirps from your mother,

that pushed you out of your nest way too young to hover, and take

flight in the wind?

I, too, fell many stories, many feet from the sky in search of the

glory we all yearn,

but you live and learn. "Patient," I said to the Baby Bird, "You'll

soon have your turn."

"Chirp-chirp-chirp," he responded, or at least that's what I thought,

until I examined his damaged wing that appeared to be caught

by his clumsiness of trying to flee. Now it's entangled in a twig,

I laughed and replied, "Baby Bird that's exactly how I lived.

My wings are my arms and they remained in cuffs,

Just the thought of flying, for me, was never enough.

I had to play with death, reaching feats never met,

I had to soar to heights that would take one's breath.

"Chirp-chirp-chirp," Baby Bird responded,

or at least that's what I thought,

Until the fear buried deep in his eyes was

that of a prey that had been caught.

"Oh no!" I exclaimed, "I'm not out to hurt you!"

"My goal is to warn you that patience is a virtue."

So as I placed Baby Bird in my palm and held him, my

arms extended to air and opportunity and nature's light,

the sun smiled radiant beams of joy as Baby Bird took flight.

But not before turning his head and giving one last, Chirp-chirp-chirp."

I guess that was his way of telling me, "Now you get up from the dirt...

And FLY!

CHAPTER 4

Is It Me Or Them?

"If you can separate and divide a community, you can conquer that community."

Phillip White

Tribal.   I think we can all relate to the definition of this word, "tribe." The *Merriam-Webster Dictionary* defines a tribe as 1) "a social group comprising numerous families, clans, or generations" and 2) "a group of persons having a common character, occupations, or interest."   In one way or another, we all have a tribal mentality whether it is with religion, political parties, wealth class, city, town, neighborhood, street organization or gang. We choose a side to support and show our allegiance and loyalty to it.   Even in our families we see this separation with favorite aunties, cousins, or a group of family members who disassociate themselves with another group for whatever reasons.   One reason is wealth or class.   If you have members in the family who are considered poor or below the poverty line, more than likely they will not be closely associated with the part of the family who has money or is considered middle or upper class.   It is a variety of reasons from which these issues arise. On one hand you have the upper class relatives who may look down on the lower class relatives and assume they are jealous of the lifestyle they live. On the other hand you have the lower class relatives who may feel as if it is the upper class relatives who are acting funny as if though they are better than the lower class relatives. These types of tribal-like issues can cause families to separate into divisions; usually causes the older relatives such as the grand-parents, great-uncles and great-aunties to come up with reasonable solutions to bring family back together. This is just one example.

Then you have the neighborhoods we live in. Almost every town or city has neighborhoods that consist of street organizations or what some may classify as "gangs." These individuals are our sons, daughters, nephews, nieces and grandchildren. Most of these young men and women were raised by me and you. We literally changed their Pampers! But as they got older they chose a group of young men to associate with and to give their allegiance and loyalty to. On the next street over you have the same scenario. The only difference is the young men on the next street may have grown up with the young men they are at odds with. Truth of the matter is they may even be related. It's not rare in this day and age to find family members in two separate street organizations that don't see eye-to-eye. I've personally run into a few brothers who don't associate with a cousin or a brother simply because "he fuck with them suckas so I don't fuck wit him." It's sad because some of these feuds, which resulted in deaths, have split families in half. But, what about the members who are not family and friends and they just feud based off of colors and streets (neighborhoods)? These individuals find themselves in a feud which may never end for generations to come. For one to judge these individuals would be foolish; beyond foolish; ignorant. Why? You ask. Well look at it this way, have you walked in the shoes of some of these young men? Do you know their story? Do you know why they chose the group of men they're hanging with? Do you think they just woke up one day and started representing an organization for no reason? Have you ever considered the fact that for many, this is their way of life? These are the circumstances they had to live in and survive under.

Some people have choices in life and others don't. Every young man can't play basketball, football, win a spelling bee or make the honor roll. Every black household doesn't have the next Tupac Shakur or Serena Williams. You do have a percentage of individuals who really have it hard in life. They come from the impossible where it is almost impossible to make it without using survival tactics they were groomed and molded with from birth. Who are you to judge them? Instead of judging them, try finding out a way to encourage them to be all they can be and not allow their circumstance to define who they are. If you are not willing to make that sacrifice then keep your opinions to yourself and enjoy your perfect life. The purpose of this book isn't to bash or drag anyone through the mud. This book has one purpose: to build what Willie Lynch thought he destroyed — your mind and way of thinking. This tribal mentality has us fighting a war within ourselves that was lost before it started. Why don't you like him? Why do you hate her? You see someone that you don't deal with and that's the first thing that comes out of your mouth. "I don't like them." But why? I'm sure we all have our reasons, but are yours reasonable? Are they sufficient enough? Not for me, but for you. You are the one who must live with your decisions. Unless you've never wronged anyone in your life, who are you to judge without mercy and forgiveness? If you are supposed to be religious, whether Christian, Muslim, Buddhist, Catholic, or whatever your preference is, you have a bigger duty to forgive those who have wronged you. The god you serve speaks high volumes to forgiving thy brother and not judging thy neighbor.

Now let's be realistic. I know it's hard to forgive someone who has hurt you and as a result traumatically scarred you, but at some point you must move on and not allow that poison to build up in you so much that you get sick and suffer mental and physical pains from not forgiving them. Never give someone that much power over you. This is also addressed to those who have lost loved ones to gang feuds and other violent acts. I can understand why the vengeance would be there in your heart. I, too, would feel some kind of revenge in my heart if one of my dear loved ones was assaulted, murdered or victimized by someone I considered my enemy, and even worse, someone I didn't know. But at some point in my life I would have to let it go in order to move on with my life. What are we to do? Are we to try and avenge the death of our loved one by killing any and everybody the perpetrator is affiliated with? Although that may seem justified at the time of your emotional breakdown, once you gather your thoughts together you will come back to reality. If you are a father, how do you keep your allegiance and loyalty to your son who looks just like you and your daughter who sounds just like you when she snores? How do you call your mother collect from jail and explain to her you are facing a murder charge while she is going through remission for her breast cancer? It's time to realize the enemy is not me and you; it's your thought process. It is filled with poison.

Instead of helping each other reach the ultimate goal of success, we'd rather discourage, put down, or hate on each other. Then with that tribal mentality, it doesn't make the situation any better because we are even quicker to lash out and say, "That's not my partner, or home-girl, or I got my own issues to worry about." It's gotten to the point where it is normal to see separatism in our communities and amongst family and associates. Although I don't want to get too far off the subject, when you look at the awards shows and voting arrangements, you can clearly see that votes are based on what class of people you are affiliated with; black or white.

The New Willie Lynch   Concrete Walls & Steel Bars
Mr. P. D. White

Look at the Oscars. It took Halle Berry getting penetrated by a Caucasian award winning actor in order for her to receive an Oscar which is looked at in the entertainment world as the "award of all awards." Then you have Denzel Washington, a black entertainer who, before playing a crooked officer in Training Day, played the role of Malcolm X. But instead of an Oscar for the better role (which was Malcolm X) he won an Oscar for playing a dirty, black cop in Los Angeles at a time when most would consider L.A. to be the focus of corrupt police officers. My example shows that unless you are considered "one of the boys or girls," then in this day and age you are the black sheep; you are blackballed; or you are on the outside looking in. This is just not in the communities where we live. This is in our homes, in the entertainment world and even in government political parties. We will discuss the role politics play in the next pages, but the higher the class and pay rate, the more you will find people with a Republican frame of mind: Tribalism.

When you look at politics, rarely will you find Democrats with the same views and opinions as Republicans. When you look at the topics discussed in politics it appears that the Democrats are the voice for lower-class Americans and the Republicans are the voice for upper-class Americans. However, I've personally witnessed views change with status. I've seen people turn from being poor, rooting for Democratic laws, opinions and presidential candidates to becoming successful, gaining wealth and frowning down at the status they were once considered: poor. With status change political change occurred and those individuals moved to the Republican side. You have entertainers from the projects and ghettos of America who once respected the support of Democrats and their laws which were structured to help lower-class individuals on welfare and needed government assistance. It was as if "as long as I'm poor I'm all for helping me get to where I need to be in life." But once they became wealthy and public figures with influence, their views changed to, "I believe you should get off your ass and work. My tax dollars are paying for your government assistance." Eventually, they ended up with a Republican opinionated state-of-mind. It's as if they forgot where they came from and the struggle they endured. Once a new class of individuals accepted them and took them in they disowned their original roots.

Could this be looked at as tribalism? Yes, of course it can. With all due respect, you have the right to choose whatever political party you desire. But unless you understand the laws each party is pushing, don't become so judgmental and quick to jump ship. Investigate what is being said to you. This is a skill that many people fail to use. It is wise to investigate what you are being told instead of being so naïve you will believe everything someone is telling you. When people debate, they usually avoid topics they have no proof of or supporting documents to verify its actuality. So a word to the wise — research and investigate what you are being told, or even worse, sold.

Sometimes we tend to follow the roads which are taken by the mass majority without investigating why everyone has chosen that route. In society today, we are accustomed to trends. Look at Twitter. If you "like" someone on Twitter you are considered a "follower." It's as if the new movement is to do what everyone else is doing. With tribes you see the same thing: "If you can't beat them, join them." There a lot of individuals who are looking for their place in life; they have no belongings; drifters who are undecided on their destiny and are willing to just roll with the flow. This is how many young African-Americans become fascinated with street organizations. This is why so many are eager to join and sign up without first looking at the stipulations or viewing the "gangsta contract" which they are about to sign. It's the need to be a part of some movement or tribe. Who wants to be on the outside looking in? No one wakes up and chooses to be a loner. Today, the world revolves around the opinions of others and being accepted. Suicide, especially from cyber-bullying, is at an all-time high due to that tribal mentality I've discussed this entire chapter. You're either in or out, accepted or rejected. Tribalism.

Leadership. When you think about that word what comes to your mind? Is it the President of the United States? Or maybe some mob boss? What about the preacher at your church? All can be considered leaders. And with leadership comes responsibility.

You have a duty to lead the people who look up to you in the right direction. But leaders tend to push the tribalism mentality onto the people who follow them and because of their loyalty to the person appointed as leader, more than likely they will inherit the leader's beliefs or dislikes towards a particular person, place or thing. If you are considered a leader or team captain, you must be careful that you don't allow your opinions and beliefs towards a particular issue or thing to become the same opinions of your team or group members. What you will end up with is a circle of individuals who can't think for themselves or bring anything to the table because they are looking to you to make all the decisions and have all the answers. What happens when you find yourself in a position where you are blinded, whether it's mentally, emotionally or physically? How can you depend on the blind to lead the blind? What do you expect a group of followers to do when the head is discombobulated?

It's time we enlighten and teach the ones who look up to us how to be leaders and make rational decisions. It's time that we take the chains off of each other and allow people to be all that they can be; to be all that God created them to be and not who you want them to be! A lot of young men and women are held in bondage by the same people they call their friends. You have a lot of decisions being made based upon what people think their friends will think. A majority of young people don't even have their own space and freedom to make decisions, but a lot of this is due to their dedication to a particular tribe. Deep inside they may feel like they want to break free and go to school to apply themselves to study. But they have "friends" discouraging them and making a mockery of their decisions to travel a positive route. So what do they do? They continue to move in a direction which is unhealthy for them.

Now this is where the negativity of tribalism comes into play and you're not able to be your own man or woman; not having the freedom to make your own decisions. Unless you move up in the ranks, you will be at the bottom of the totem pole trying to impress those that really mean you no good. It's like a game of chess. You put your pawns on the first row because they usually get sacrificed at the beginning of the game and therefore the other pieces can make moves beneficial to the king. When you are playing a skilled player, it's unlikely that the pawn will move up in rank and get to enjoy the luxury of becoming a rook, bishop, horse or queen, even though it does happen. My point is this — a lot of individuals who think they are part of an organization, group or tribe are really nothing more than collateral for the true leader in power. At anytime you can be used, thrown away or have your spot taken by the next blind and naïve person who wants to be accepted. It's time to become your own man and woman and make decisions which will benefit you and your family in a positive way. If at the end of the day you feel you have no voice in the circle you dedicate yourself to, more than likely you don't.

The New Willie Lynch   Concrete Walls & Steel Bars
Mr. P. D. White

Earlier this year a group of individuals and I were having a discussion in one of my creative writing classes. One individual did a spoken work piece on Martin Luther King, Jr. and his opinions were based upon what he felt Martin Luther King Jr.'s role was in black history. At the end of his performance there was a brief and heated debate where one brother said, "Okay, with all that being said, "What are you doing to change the problem?" The room got quiet. I spoke up and said, "I'm in the process of publishing a book based on Willie Lynch's programming of the Negro. I can't speak for everyone else but I dedicated my time toward educating those around me and helping the community I am responsible for destroying." It wasn't what he said that got the response I gave. It was how he said it, as if there weren't any real men who were willing to take a stand and push for what they believed in. I respect his approach, because you do have a lot of "talkers" and not enough "walkers" who are willing to fight for the rights of their community. But we must get out of the mentality of attempting to doubt others who are ready to take a stand on injustice.

The power is with the people and the people are me and you. If the links in our foundation are weakened by weak-minded individuals who have already given up on themselves, what makes you think they will fight for you and me? You got leaders in positions of power who shouldn't have the positions they are in. Either they bullied their way into their positions, used money and status to gain it, or used trickery. But a lot of people just have titles to their names which they don't deserve. They are misleading people and need to be removed from their positions so real standup individuals can take over and lead the movement of positive progress in the direction it needs to go. It's common to see someone in a position of power abuse their authority by misguiding others and taking advantage of the loyalty others have for them. You see it in almost everything where power is involved; whether it's law enforcement, government, prison officials, sports, entertainment, Wall Street, etc. You even see it in churches and religious communities where you should feel safe and protected from the evils outside of your beliefs. In the *New King James Bible* version there is a scripture which warns leaders and teachers: "My brethren (brother), let not many of you become teachers, knowing that we shall receive a stricter judgment" (James 3:1). This reference is in a study Bible which breaks down the translation of the scripture as teachers being judged more strictly by God during Judgment Day. Their greater influence translates into greater responsibility.

Leadership imposes responsibility. So leaders must be very careful when carrying the torch with a flock of people following them and believing in them and their vision. If you want to travel down the road of destruction go right ahead, but don't take someone else with you. It's not righteous for them and the future they may want to have. Being in control is more than just giving orders and making rational decisions.   You are still held accountable for your choices because the people you lead are a reflection of you.

I recently interviewed a young African-American male and the first question I asked him was, "If you could change one thing about your past what would it be?" He paused and reflected on the question. Before he answered he reminded me that he had been incarcerated for the past fifteen years. This was also someone I looked at as an older, responsible adult who held a positive leadership role for younger black men who came to him for advice. After a few seconds of pondering the question he replied, "My biggest mistake was extending my loyalty." I asked him to briefly go into deeper detail about what he meant. He went on to say, "I involved myself with too much unnecessary association, and not recognizing the men who were assets and the ones who were liabilities to me and my future." I agreed that this was the case with many other men that I interviewed in prison who felt they were obligated to associate with a certain group of individuals based on race, religion, or city, town and hoods where they once lived. A majority recognized that the love they received was given to them by individuals they never grew up with, never knew and never would have even spoken to them on the streets due to their allegiance and loyalty to a particular organization or group of people. Tribalism.

This is a subject which can be broken down into many subchapters and discussed on many levels. It is important that you remind yourself: "In order to break my own ways and reprogram my way of thinking, I must rid myself of the tribal mentality." You are your own enemy. You will be surprised at how many doors will open for you once you learn to extend your hand to those around you. The old saying, "Don't judge a book by its cover," is true. Don't judge it by its color or neighborhood either.

Last Night I Smacked Some Girl
By Mr. P. D. White

To my Mom, Grandma, Daughter, Sister and women across the world,

please forgive me, but last night I smacked some girl.

I didn't know her. I just drove to some inner city corner, jumped out my car,

said a few words to the man she belonged to and rode off with her.

As we rode through the city I told her my life story, or at least the chapters

I thought were relevant: how I lost my job, well, got fired; how everything

I ever did just never worked out. She listened, not once did she interrupt me.

She began to talk to me. Her voice gave me butterflies in my stomach.

She reminded me of this other girl I knew. She told me where she was from.

I can't recall the exact location, but I'm sure it was somewhere in Mexico.

Her English was broken and, although she sounded foreign, she was paler than the coke-
white leather seats in my old Caddy Coupe Deville. Yeah, last night I smacked some girl.

I didn't even apologize either. Once we pulled up to some old raggedy hole-in-the-
wall motel, I aggressively yanked her out the car and said, "Come on!"
She put up no fight. Before I knew it I was holding her caressing her, looking at her
gown which was clear and see-through, Hmmmm-mmm-ummm!

The mounds on this woman had my mouth watering, anxiety ran through my body
as my nose began to also run. Instantly I embraced her. She embraced me even tighter,
so tight she caused my veins to bulge out. She gave me a head-rush. My body got warm.
I began to sweat. Last night I smacked some girl. She was so good, Hmmm-mmm.

We laughed, talked, cried, damn…this was the first woman that made me open up.

Actually once I got started , I couldn't stop talking. Sex so good I had to fire up a

Newport 100… Yeah, last night I smacked some girl.

Before we left the motel room I begged for one last taste of her love…

She said, "Of course, Big Daddy." The last thrust was so strong she made

my heart EXPLODE!!

CHAPTER 5
The Never-Ending Dope Game

"Insane is the act of doing something over and over and expecting a different result."
Wise old saying

Once you're locked into the dope game, it's hard to find a key to let you out. The average African-American male who jumps off the porch and is loosed into the world of hustling knows that when they sign a contract to join the "dope game" it ends with them either in prison, or hooked on dope, or paralyzed from the consequences of the game, or death. Very few make it out of the "dope game." To many it is just that, a game. But it is really no game at all. It is more like a serious roll of the dice where the probability of rolling seven or eleven is very unlikely. It's not only dangerous but very addictive for those who do experience the luxury of accumulating a large amount of money, possessions and success. The fame alone can be considered more addictive than the money itself. Just the thought of being accepted or needed is enough to push a young, poor African-American kid who is living in poverty to pick up a dope sack and start his journey on the road to riches...or ditches. There comes a lot of unwanted stress and habits with the dope game. The stress can be connected to once you move up the ladder of success you are now called upon to take care of more responsibility. It seems as if everyone needs something from the big man at the top. Not only do you have to worry about the leeches in your family, but the jealous and envious homies, police, snitches, baby mama drama, and the jack boys, i.e., the Robin Hoods who "steal from the rich and give to the poor."

Also, the pros and cons of the dope game are severe; on both ends the good and the bad. There really is no good that comes out of the dope game unless you are one of those people who do eventually climb the ladder high enough to where you are fortunate enough to provide for those less fortunate. But even that has its pros and cons, especially when you do exit the game, only to have your past thrown up in your face and the media. You must be very careful when you enter into this land of the scandalous. This game has no friends and only casualties. When I speak from the dope game perspective I speak from hands-on experience. I grew up believing that in order to provide for my family I had to sale dope. At the time it was true because I was only 12 years of age. And what job can a 12 year old child obtain that is sufficient enough to help pay bills? Cutting grass just wasn't going to do it, especially when your neighbors are all project tenants.

In the beginning, my reason for being drafted into the dope game was simple: to help my mother who had two other mouths to feed. But what happens when you pass the stage of providing for your loved ones? You are now all in and hooked like a big-mouthed bass. Now you must use what you've learned—as a means to survive—to accommodate your other needs such as cars, clothes, jewelry, women and other things except your original objective of providing for your family. Your way of life changes to the point where you must continue to indulge in something as negative as the dope game, in order to keep up with your new lifestyle. Anytime you progress in life, whether in your career as a sports player, entertainer, actor or drug dealer, you get accustomed to the finer things in life. You inherit expensive tastes. You pick up new priorities and new bills. It now becomes a must to keep up your image and reputation. The further you get into the game, the more you suffocate yourself and cut off your lifeline. You are not only poisoning your community in which you push your product, you are also mentally poisoning yourself. You have now voluntarily made yourself a product of your environment.

We can all go back decades and even centuries to the root of the problem. In the minds of many the problem is the government. That topic alone is a whole other book. But who do you blame once you are wide awake and you understand the cause and effect of your actions? Who do you point the finger at when you move out of the ghetto, relocate to the suburbs and only return to the ghetto to push your dope? Who is forcing you to do that? Honestly? Who is telling you to re-up them for 2 or 3 kilos? Who is telling you to go into your stash spot of $50,000 or more and cop those rims which will set you back $10,000 and put you in a position where you must re-up and take the risk of getting incarcerated for distribution or possibly robbed and killed in a drug transaction gone bad. Sometimes we just don't know when to quit. We tell ourselves "one more trip and I'm done" when that last trip could actually be our last.

Drug dealers are just as bad as the drug users, if not worse. The drug user knows who he is and what he's addicted to. He looks in the mirror and sees his self-destruction. The drug dealer doesn't usually see his self-destructive ways until it's too late. He's either in a jail cell, on a hospital bed, strung out, in debt, in the trunk of someone's car being held for ransom, or on his deathbed. The warning signs are there, but the common sense you're born with is not kicking in quick enough. Even when the common sense and intuition kicks in, you may continue to lie and deny the risk-level of your actions. It's easy to water down our situations and downplay them so we can feel comfortable with the decisions we make. But the truth of the matter is you will only drown in the pool of lies that you throw on yourself. Where is your float? You better know how to swim because in the dope game it gets deep. Like Young Jeezy said, "How deep? Deep as the abyss."

You got the sharks in the water and not all of them wear blue suits and shiny badges. Some of them look just like you and me. Literally, just like YOU! You are your own shark in your own ocean of life. Are you so greedy that you're willing to eat yourself in order to survive? That is exactly what is being done anytime you put any substance in the palm of your hands and step on the yellow brick road to riches in pursuit of happiness. You probably have a greater chance of taking a new .357 revolver, placing three shells into it and pulling the trigger three times without ending up with a slug in your head. Reality is one thing many people choose not to deal with. Why? Well I have yet to find out the answer to that. One thing I can inform you about is this: life is more than the fabricated lies we've been told growing up about the dope game being the only option for a young black man in the inner-city ghettos of the United States of America. Although it has its benefits like any career you put your heart into, the downside outweighs the benefits. The truth is it's not worth it. This is my belief and opinion. I do understand the cards you must play in life in order to survive and walk through the storms and tornados, but you must also consider the future consequences and impacts which come with the decisions you've made.

Life does have the tendency to back you so far into a corner that you have to fight dirty in order to get out of that corner. I've witnessed the dope game ruin not only family and the best of friends, but generations have been destroyed behind the dope game. Futures have ("poof") gone up in smoke; dreams shattered like glass windows in the middle of an earthquake. The magnitude of destruction that the dope game causes is far beyond 100 on the

Richter scale. You have the senseless murders in our communities over turfs and territory in the dope game. In these shootouts that occur over "spots" or "traps" you have multiple innocent kids and adults who suffer because of some reckless individual who wants to stake his claim on something which never belonged to him in the first place. It's sad when our youths can't enjoy the luxury of playing in their front yard for fear of being hit by a stray bullet from a high-powered rifle. It's even sadder when they wonder "Why can't I go outside and play?"

People, it's time we wake our game up. I don't crucify the players in the dope game. How can I? I was that same blind, young boy on the corner just trying to carry my end in this thing we all call "life." It's not easy. It never is simple when you consider the fact that many of us come into this world with the cards already stacked against us. What do you say to a 12-year old child who has to watch his mother struggle with a drug addiction, pay the bills and feed his other siblings in the home? What advice can you offer him? From a religious point of view you could encourage him to pray. But what happens when a child prays so much that his throat becomes sore, his dignity is broken and he feels as if God doesn't look at him as a equal to the kids he sees on TV in nice homes and communities? It's not hard to discourage a child no matter how irrational you may think their decisions are.

We are living as victims being victimized by other victims. We are hurting so badly that we will go out of our way to hurt others so we can feel better.   And it's not always intentional. Really, who wakes up as a child and tells himself "I want to sell dope to destroy homes and generations and tear down my community." I doubt a child would think in those sick ways. The average kid just wants to put a little food on the table, help around the house and maybe buy a nice pair of Jordans — in the beginning. But once they discover the role they'll play in the game has more benefits than just that first $100.00 dollars they made, from that point on they enter into the tunnel of "no return." They are mentally and emotionally locked in what I describe as "the never-ending dope game." So as you read this you might be telling yourself "Okay, I know all of this; tell me something I don't know." My rebuttal is this, "If you know all of this and have enough common sense to decipher reality from fiction, are you ready to take a stand?" We must start educating our children at a young age that no matter how hard life may seem they cannot allow their circumstances to hurt others.   The drug trade dope game has no winners, only losers.   The addicts lose and the hustlers lose if and when the game ends for them whether through prison, becoming an addict or death by consequences of the game. Eventually, it all comes to a halt.

There are a few major players who get lucky and make it out. My advice to them is to "give back." And not give to just a few toy and food drives but rebuild those communities they destroyed.   Consider building some youth centers, buying some homes and putting homeless families into them, free of charge, until they can get on their feet. Open up a childcare center where jobless parents can get assistance with their needs until they are employed. Start some non-profit organizations which are centered on helping the same communities you helped destroy. All it takes is a will to want to change. Even in the Bible it speaks about those who steal to feed their family as a righteous cause. The Bible doesn't encourage anyone to steal. However, the Bible does say it's understandable and under those terms after you have accumulated the funds to pay back those you've stolen from, you must return the favor "sevenfold." The actual Bible reference says, "People, *do not* despise a thief if he steals to satisfy himself when he is starving, yet when he is found, he must restore sevenfold: he may have to give up all the substance of his house" (Proverbs 6:30-31).

I definitely don't want my readers to think I'm just making up a bunch of parables or mumbo jumbo. The reality of it is to give back. There is more than one way to give. It doesn't necessarily have to be money. You can give back by starting Peewee league football and basketball teams. Open a local barbershop and run weekly functions out of it to give back to the community. Just don't become someone who took from the poor and gave to the rich. And if you need that broken down into simple English, don't destroy your neighborhood and move to the suburbs and bathe in your luxury while the community you've destroyed is left behind to try to pick up the pieces and rebuild again; drowning in the catastrophe you created. My advice to the young brother who is faced with the decision to either enter the eternal dope game or is forced to starve, is to keep going to school (if you are in school) and educate yourself. Don't let your status as a victim cause you to victimize and hurt others. There are many young men and women who are in worse environments than you are in but they made it out.

Every circumstance is different and unique and there are other options you can consider, even at the young ages of 12 and 13 years old. You can start a small movement in your community with other young men and voice your needs and opinions online via YouTube, Facebook, Twitter, etc. and request that the Congressman and political leaders in your town or city step-up and do something about your living conditions. Start a "Go Me Fund" that is geared towards getting a youth football or basketball team in your area. Start a campaign for a youth center, arcade or library. Push. Don't stop at the location on the monopoly board that reads "The Dope Game" because once you pick up those dice there's no guarantee you'll be among the lucky ones to actually make it out to retire. Live your life; shoot for the stars. The images you see on those BET (Black Entertainment Television) videos are 90% watered down. Yes, there is a lifestyle where you can inherit cars, clothing, money and women, but at what cost?

Let me ask the young people reading this book a question. Do you know what a slave master is? Do you know what their duty is? Are you considered a slave master if you take a group of people and promise them something in return for their services and hard labor? So is it safe to say that when a hustler pushes his product on the people in his community for a small price he is considered a slave master? Especially when people will do almost any and everything to get the product for that little freedom of feeling "high" and "relaxed." This is just as bad as slavery. The only thing different is that you are selling false hope at a discount price and may even give it away on credit. Young world don't be fooled by the glitter and bling. There's a dark side to a life of shining. A lot of rappers don't tell you this. They won't reveal the true effects of the dope game.

And the effects don't always end in prison and death. What happens when you inherit paranoia or a personality disorder or you become anti-social? The game is structured to turn you into something larger than life. However, every drug has a side-effect. Yes, the dope game is like a very addictive drug with a disturbing side-effect. It's not hard to understand why you would lose your mind once you entered a game you didn't really know the full details about. Did you read the fine print before signing your life away on the contract? Did you perform your research on the consequences of the game, or did you just jump in blindfolded with hopes of copping that new Lamborghini you saw in that new rap video? Whatever your reasons and desires are I can tell you from hands-on experience, it rarely ends with happy faces and Hallmark cards. The dead ends of the dope game have trapped many young men and women behind bars and in graveyards.

It is easy to give up and quit and take the route which appears the easiest. Character is built when you go against the odds you are given and break the chains which bind you. Put your mind towards something positive and constructive to succeed. Many look at their current situations and already assume life will end tragically for them so they throw in the towel and play into the hands of negativity. Having faith is only half the answer. You must also work; that is, along with faith and prayer you must use what God has given you and apply yourself. God equipped you with hands, feet and a brain to think with. He gave you eyes to see and ears to hear. If you are put in the position where you are unfortunate and can't use one of the former, it is always good to keep an optimistic view and speak positive things into existence. The never-ending dope game is being played at an all-time high. It is no longer an issue in the urban ghettos of America; it is an issue all over the country, including those gated communities we find ourselves running to once we are fortunate enough to make it out of the ghetto. The drug tolerance for drug users increases with every new drug. Even older drugs have resurfaced and become popular again as major drugs of choice.

Our youths are in search of something to relieve them of their pains and worries. The first thing many run to is that which is easy to access: drugs. Which drug they choose to indulge in is more or less based upon their peers and surroundings. If the circle of individuals they associate with use marijuana then it's likely they will become curious enough to try it at least once. If they find themselves in the presence of peers who use more potent drugs such as crystal meth, cocaine, Ecstasy, Mollies, syrup, heroin shrums, acid, PCP and LSD, then you have a major problem on your hands because teens enjoy the feeling of being accepted and appearing as being "cool" to their peers. This is an epidemic which the government has yet to find a cure for.

And entertainers don't make it any easier. These are the same people our children look up to as role models and they brag about using drugs as if it's the cool thing to do if you want to be someone important. Our youth are being brainwashed into believing that negativity is the new positive. You rarely see people around you encouraging you to strive for greatness. And for teens it's more of a need to do the opposite which is to strive for a fictional lifestyle which has been scripted on our TV screens and in our music, which is that of a boss or a bad bitch. The basic promotion says, "If you a bad bitch you need the man on big rims, with big money and making big moves." The other side says, "If you're a boss you must ride big rims, wear the big chain, drive the most expensive car and these things will give you fame and the women." But it's all at the selling price of your soul to the dope game. These things can all be accumulated by hard work and effort but many people want these rewards of life to come overnight. This means they will probably indulge in something illegal such as the dope game so they can obtain these things.

The dope game is a gateway to many things I wouldn't wish on my worst enemy. Even the biggest players who have been in the game a long time want out. But how do you walk away from something which gives you the things you need to survive in life? How do you walk away from your day job and expect to keep up your image and still pay bills and provide for those around you who are now use to the finer things in life? These are questions I can't answer for the players in the game. Through the pain and suffering they will eventually wake up and choose a different route in life other than the one which leads down a path of destruction. When you do exit the game—if you are fortunate enough to be free and unmarked with all your screws still intact—it would be wise of you to warn others about the pros and cons of the game, sharing the dark side with them. Tell them about all the nights you couldn't sleep for fear of your door being kicked in; or how you lived life through your rearview mirror, thinking every car that passed you with tints was an undercover agent; and how you inherited bad nerves just thinking about the safety of your family. These are just a few, small, minor things that people who have played the game can share with the rookies entering the off-season draft and are eager to come off the bench and earn a name for themselves. Once you put those Jordans on be ready to lace 'em up tight because you've got a tough game ahead of you to play, kid — the never-ending dope game. Game over!

Look at the most drug-infested neighborhoods in America. A large percentage of them are located in highly populated black communities. Right across the street from these communities are liquor stores which provide both the drug dealers and drug users with the necessities needed to carry out their agendas. You got your beer, wine, cigars (blunts), lottery tickets, glass pipes, etc. Liquor stores attract winos, prostitutes and drug peddlers to their parking lots which play into the violence these neighborhoods grow accustomed to. The traffic alone is enough to stir up confusion. These poverty-stricken communities are fighting a war not only on drugs but also gangs, prostitution, police brutality, racial profiling and the reality that there are liquor stores which push and promote poison. How do you escape a jungle full of negativity right outside your front door?

When you drive across town to the suburban communities you feel as if you've entered an entirely different world. You won't see a squad of police vehicles circling the streets; there are no liquor stores with solicitations going on in their parking lot by prostitutes, drug pushers and drug buyers; and the streets aren't littered with drug paraphernalia, dirty syringes, empty shells from a shootout, empty coke bags with residue on them, used condoms and just trash. If we begin to take inventory on where we reside and the surroundings in which our children call home, we would get pissed off with the thought of living in filth. There is no other word to describe some of the neighborhoods we live in. This should be an eye-opening opportunity for those who are tired of living in circumstances even poor families in Haiti don't live in.

However, there is something we can do. We can blow the whistle on this disturbing movie script straight out of a Donald Goins book. It's time to huddle up the team players and real leaders and call it quits in this never-ending dope game which has so many of our children and loved ones living in a real life resident evil, grand theft auto type of lifestyle. Do you have someone you love that has been affected by the consequences of playing in the never-ending dope game? Do you have a son, daughter, grandchild, brother or sister that is doing time in prison for a drug-related offense? Do you have a loved one who is addicted to a particular drug and has given up on hope? Do you pray so much that you sometimes feel as if it's no use? Do you ask yourself, "When will this child wake up and realize they are walking on a tightrope over hell blindfolded?" Does music that glorify drug-dealing and poverty disturb and frustrate you? Do you ever ride past the local liquor store on the corner and wonder "what do these fools do all day other than hang out?" The never-ending dope game was created to do just that; to keep the players occupied with trying to play for false hope.

The New Willie Lynch   Concrete Walls & Steel Bars
Mr. P. D. White

Once the crack epidemic hit the ghettos of America, you had three group of players: the dealers who would distribute the product to make their lives better; the buyers who would purchase the product to relieve life's stress; and law enforcement (government) who pledges to protect and serve, but instead are self-employees who distribute the product and charge the taxpayers a hefty price to incarcerate local small-time drug dealers who move the product their superiors initially provided them with. In other words, it's all a big game. The mob used the same tactics. Send some goons to a local store, have them tear it up, destroy the goods and take whatever money is in the cash register and safe. Now you have frightened store owners who don't know what to do. For the next two weeks you perform the same routine. After about the third time, you send a respected figure of the community into the store. He promises the store owner protection for a small monthly percentage of the store's earnings. To prove to the store owner that his security methods will work, he calls his goons off for the next three weeks — peace and quiet. The store owner now feels he'd rather pay a small fee and have protection rather than have his store destroyed weekly, lose customers and continue to give up large amounts of cash from the register. We call this extortion. But when you do it behind a badge and contracts it's called legal extortion.

The government puts the dope on the streets which is the cause of a spike in violence. Then they promise taxpayers if they vote to fund new police programs and prison laws, they can clean the streets up and make the city a safer place. Extortion. If there is no dope in the hoods, the crime rate decreases, which means law enforcement lose money and can't afford to pay the police force. This means less prisoners going to prison which means the shutdown of billion dollar prison facilities that can no longer fill up bed space to house prisoners. For those of you who play the game you are keeping these same people you call corrupt, employed. The longer you play right into their little game of survival, the longer you keep them employed. They don't eat unless we feed them.

If you do your research you will find out that African-Americans built this country before the dope game was ever heard of. We invented some of the most useful and influential inventions. We are natural born thinkers, craftsmen and entrepreneurs. Our intellect level is sometimes underrated and overlooked. If you look at some of the most dominant athletes you can contribute their legacies to their intellectual knowledge of the particular sport they play. To be honest, African-Americans dominate every popular sport other than hockey; and it won't be long before we see the next Michael Jordan of hockey out there on the ice. We are some of the best entertainers, actors, musicians, etc. It's time we look at the bigger picture and start educating our youth and the next generation about the importance of education and doing the right thing, no matter the cost. No child wants to sit back and watch their family struggle to put food on the table and pay bills. There is almost always an urge to be the breadwinner in the household which saves the family from drowning and going under. But our children must be warned about the severe consequences of participating in the never-ending dope game. If you are a parent who is in a fortunate position to provide for your children, make sure you don't overly provide. Teach them about morals and the power of the dollar. Mold them into independent young adults who know the art of saving money. Therefore, when they earn it they won't find themselves entering the dope game in a rush to get a little extra money.

It's time that we all take responsibility for each other; each one, teach one. We have the power to shift the direction our communities are moving. We can't sit back and talk about it. There's no reason to sit back and cry about it. It's time to be productive and do something about it. People feel like "I'm just one little person so how can I change the world by myself?" Well, your focus shouldn't be to try to change the world. First, you focus on changing the person you are for the better and then you work on encouraging others around you to do the same. Once you have progressed in creating a positive surrounding of individuals who are likeminded then you can put your thoughts together and come up with a solution to fix whatever issue it is that needs to be fixed or addressed. Sometimes it's easier to be discouraged rather than encouraged. Just the thought of going against the "grain" or what is popular can cause someone to divert their agenda elsewhere. We need more leaders in our communities. We need more people who are willing to take a stand for what is right and repair what is wrong.

Where are our morals? Are we so afraid of our own children that we neglect to raise them properly and apply discipline where it is needed? Are we so exhausted we've merely given up on our community and now we just accept the living standards? Are we so naïve that we just sit back and allow our loved ones to destroy each other? When do we act as men and women with integrity and character and say, "Enough is enough?" I can't do it for you. I can want it for you but you must want it for yourself so badly that you get up and do something. All it takes is a drop of ink on a clean sheet of paper to change it from being blank to a sheet of paper with a blemish from a drop of ink on it. So apply that to life. All it takes is one small effort to get the positive ball rolling and you'll be surprised at how many others feel exactly the same way. You are not alone in your struggles.

We all strive for some kind of ultimate goal whether it is negative or positive. It's time to use that built-up energy for something constructive rather than destructive. No matter how much good you may think comes out of the dope game, lives are ruined by the millions! It is a negative outlet for those who only want to do positive things for themselves and their loved ones. It's sad that in order to find some sense of peace and happiness people will stoop to the level of selling drugs in their own community. Does anyone stop to consider what people will do to get these drugs? Many kill, steal, rob and do treacherous things to feed the monkey on their backs. Then you have pregnant mothers who feed their urge to get high during pregnancy which destroys the child inside of her. It's a never-ending ball of confusion. I could go on and on with scenarios: The mother who gives up all of her food stamps to get high; the father who spends his entire check for a quick blast; the man who broke into your home for Christmas to feed his need to get loaded; or the hoop-star who needed money to feed his family so he jumped into the game for a quick $100.00 dollars and ended up doing 100 years instead. It doesn't stop there and that's why it's called the never-ending dope game.

This is something that may go on and on for the next 100 years if we don't stand up and do something about it. I'm being realistic here when I say that it will not be an easy task, but anything worth having is worth fighting for. Don't you think your kids' futures are worth saving? Don't you think the freedom of the next generation is worth fighting for? Shouldn't our friends and family have the support of strong-minded leaders who are willing to fight for them? YES!

Tears

By Mr. P. D. White

My son got paralyzed. Finally he can walk again.

My homie got paralyzed. Doctors said he ain't gone

walk again…Tears.

My homie used to sell his own mama dope;

He cried tears she had a stroke;

Thank God she ain't overdose…Tears.

This brother carjacked people most his life;

Died at the yellow light;

He got carjacked last night…Tears.

I knew a guy who kidnapped for them white bricks;

Cried tears, they kidnapped his children;

Life's triflin'…Tears

You point and laugh at homeless people every day;

Lose your job, cry tears;

Now you got nowhere to stay…Tears.

The New Willie Lynch   Concrete Walls & Steel Bars
Mr. P. D. White

I cried tears, they burn and it's hard to stay strong;

Ugly is when you wake up out of a coma,

and your face is gone…Tears.

Real tears…cried so many years;

Lived in the fast lane and died

behind the steering wheel…Tears.

Neglect your kids; you just a baby father?

Break down in tears if you hear somebody

raped your daughter…Tears.

Rosa Parks, Tears Malcolm X…Tears.

Tupac Shakur died without a vest…Tears.

Eric Wright, the brother Eazy E, Eric Garner

cried out, "It's hard for me to breathe"…Tears.

Freddie Gray…Tears, Michael Brown…Tears.

Tears for the little brother who got murdered up in Chi-town;

Didn't see his teens, called it a gang murder.

We cry tears for the pain of the slain and the murdered.

Nine lives lost in South Carolina; died in church.

The New Willie Lynch   Concrete Walls & Steel Bars
Mr. P. D. White

I know Jesus cried a river bigger than China.

Drug addiction tears, battered women tears,

the world is crying tears;

We need more Kleenex for the years…Tears.

CHAPTER 6

Get Yo' Game Woke All the Way Up!

Happiness. In some form or fashion a majority of people search for this desperately. Whether we find it through shopping, praying, reading the Bible or spending time with the ones we love, happiness is good for the soul and good for our health. Stress is not only agonizing and painful but also deadly. We must be very careful at what we put our energies into. Stress can drain you emotionally and physically.   Many people find themselves stressing or in stressful situations and act-out in very irrational ways. Some bite their nails down to nubs whereas others may eat until they are so stuffed they must force themselves to vomit while others may act-out violently.

In the world today, a lot of the violence we see happening on the news across the globe in some way is probably connected to untreated stress. People simply don't have the life-skills to properly deal with stressful events. The old method of taking a deep breath and counting to ten is very effective, but only for those who use it. Growing up, I was one of those kids who acted-out when I was under a lot of stress. I was involved in a number of fights, confrontations and got in a lot of trouble simply because I didn't know how to deal with stress. We live in a very awkward world where negativity seems to be the norm. You often find yourself waking up on the good side of the bed, having a pretty decent day until you go into the office and your day is disrupted by co-workers you can't avoid. It's good not to feed into negative energy. Try to remove yourself from a negative situation at all cost. If you choose to stay and confront the issue, it could have an adverse effect which could put you in a life-changing situation. It only takes a second to make a mistake but a lifetime to get out of the mistake you made.

How many of you readers have found yourselves arguing with a customer representative on the other end of a call because they said the wrong thing or couldn't help you with your order? How many have actually argued at the drive-thru window because your food wasn't properly prepared or they just took longer than usual to serve you? How many have stood in a line at a store only to get frustrated by the person in front of you who is taking all day to check out their items? All it takes is the other person saying the wrong thing and you're instantly on the defense. If that person just so happens to feel as if you pose a threat to them, now you may risk the chance of being involved in a physical altercation.

People, we got to be smart enough to see the disaster before disaster strikes. Your gut instinct may be the most important intuition that you have. Sometimes if the circumstances just don't seem right then nine times out of ten they aren't; and there's an even bigger chance you may be the root of the problem. I say this out of respect for the power you possess to control the situation before the situation controls you. African-Americans are already perceived by many as savage animals that act-out whenever they don't get their way. Many ignorant people view the African-American race as aggressive individuals who resort to violence during any confrontation. In order to reverse this stereotype we, as a people, must start taking inventory on the things which push us over the limit and cause us unwanted stress. It's not enough to just brush it off as something you'll try to deal with when a confrontation arises. It's time to do something now.

CHAPTER 7

The Second Door to Reprogramming Your Mind

31-DAY REPROGRAMMING PROCESS

Starting My Day Off Positive

<u>**DAY 1**</u>

Starting your week off on a good positive note is just as important as starting your day off on the same note. How your day starts can be very detrimental to how your week ends up. Through the experience of having bad days and even worse weeks, I've managed to come up with a reliable solution: prayer at the beginning of each day. When I get up, instead of doing my usual routine of washing my face, brushing my teeth and getting prepared for work, I now pray when I first open my eyes. I found that by doing this, I condition my mind to be prepared for whatever struggles I may face that day. During prayer I try to block out everything around me. The television is turned off, no music is playing and I'm in a peaceful setting. After my prayer, I usually take two to three minutes to meditate and reflect on my prayer. I've been using this method of starting my day off for the past three years and the results are outstanding! It's as if anytime I'm faced with any negative energy, I reflect back on my prayer and how my day first started.

To start your day off badly can have a negative effect later on in your schedule. If you misplaced your car keys, spilled coffee on your work uniform, or didn't receive your morning newspaper, these things can have an adverse effect on how your day may end.

It's also best to try to allow positive energy to control your attitude and walk through life. Even when minor things disrupt us, it's best to have a positive attitude and continue to push forward. Smile, it works. Be thankful that you woke up to start your week off on a good note. Someone didn't have the pleasure of waking up today. Remember that. God touched you this morning for a reason, so let it be a good reason. Smile.

Advice: God chose you to help him this week. What role do you play?

-

These Three Words (I Love You)

DAY 2

These three words, "I love you," are strong enough to make the strongest person weak in the knees. Who do you love? I used to think love was a feeling that I wanted to feel forever until I realized the truth: nothing lasts forever. Eventually you will let go of someone or something you love at some point in your life. But while the people you love the most are well and breathing, use this day to tell them just how much you love them. Write them a letter, send them a text, or go online and post it on their page. Letting someone know they are loved can make the the difference between their day being a blessed day or a down one. If you got kids and they live in the same household as you do, try going into their room while they are asleep and just wake them up and tell them, "I love you." If your children aren't in your life try reaching out to them through a third party and let them know you love them. If you haven't told your fiancé or spouse you love them in a while, try telling them you love them today.

Love is a powerful form of energy that can only be shown through action. The power of communicating to someone just how much you love them can change the circumstances in their lives. A lot of people don't feel love, that's why they do awkward things and act-out. Tell your friends you are close to, "I love you." It takes even more humanity to tell an enemy, "I love you." But if you intend to move forward in life in search of peace, loving those who wronged you is a powerful first step to take. Love isn't selfish, puffed up or boisterous. Love is just good ol' fashion love. If you love the person around you on a daily basis, give them a hug today and tell them, "I love you!"

Advice: Tell someone you love them. They may not know it until you say it!

Forgiveness

DAY 3

Forgiveness. How easy is it not to forgive? Pretty easy. But to forgive someone may be the most difficult thing we do in our lifetime. Forgiveness starts with understanding that as humans, we make mistakes. It may be even harder to forgive ourselves for some wrong we've committed. But without forgiveness we allow poison to build up in us which can affect us mentally, emotionally and physically. I can recall a minor situation where I held a grudge against one of my best friends for many years. Whenever I would see him, I would purposely avoid contact with him, not wanting to give him an opportunity to apologize for the wrong he had done to me. It got to the point where anytime I would see him out and about, my stress level would increase and my blood pressure would rise. I would go home with a throbbing headache and reopened scars.

After a few years of my childish charade, I finally took the initiative to talk to him about our misunderstanding and how I felt as if he was wrong for his actions. He agreed and apologized. He informed me that he had not forgiven himself because I wouldn't forgive him. This caused him to grow into the habit of drinking excessively and using drugs which he never indulged in prior to our misunderstanding. We are the best of friends today and consult with each other when we are faced with difficult decisions to make. The act of forgiveness is the right thing to do. No one is perfect because we all fall short and make mistakes no matter how big or small they may be. Sometimes you have to be the bigger person and apologize first. You never know the bridge of communication that unselfish act can build. Today, think of someone you've had an altercation with and patch it up.

Advice: Remember, life is too short to be upset at an old friend or loved one.

Don't Be A Stranger

DAY 4

Every time my phone rings I hope it's someone I haven't talked to in a while. Just the thought of knowing someone from my past is still thinking of me or appreciates my existence is enough to get me through a rough day. Have you ever received a call from an auntie or relative you haven't spoken to in months but always wondered how they were doing? How does that letter or call you receive make you feel? I often find myself encouraging my younger friends to reach out to their relatives they haven't heard from in a long time. The response I get sometimes is, "Why? They aren't looking for me!" I respond, "They may have lost your number, contact information or they may be going through a difficult time in life and need to hear from someone close to them." The results are always positive. Usually I see their face light up when they call that person they've been out of contact with for so long.

When they receive a letter it's even a bigger prize because they read the letter over and over and find new things that the letter is saying. Sometimes our assumptions are wrong. They are based upon what we hope they are. If we feel as if someone would rather not hear from us, we allow our minds to tell us that.   We agree with our assumptions because it's an easy way out of the task of communicating with that person. Have you ever told yourself something and then pumped yourself up to believe it so you don't have to deal with a task? I think we've all done this. So today is a good day to contact someone you haven't spoken to in a while. Just send a text, card, voicemail, or pop-up at the job with lunch. You can go to your kid's school if you haven't done so in a while. Just let that person know you haven't forgotten about them. The results will amaze you.

Advice: The act of being kind is worthy of a standing ovation.

Those Who Give Blessings Receive Blessings
<u>DAY 5</u>

I've heard some of my friends say, "You're a baller." I laugh and respond by telling them, "No, I'm just blessed." In the world we live in today we have millions of unfortunate people who don't have a decent shirt to put on. I was having a conversation with a female friend who is the youth pastor of her church. She had been going through some financial difficulties and was struggling to maintain her everyday lifestyle. She told me about a guy outside of her job would who speak to her every day as she entered work and when she left. When I asked what he would say to her she said, "All he said was 'God bless you sister.'" She said he did this everyday for a year straight. She got paid later that week and told me that God told her to bless someone.

She told me she went to work as usual that day and didn't see the man when she went in or when she left. She felt as if though she was going to miss the opportunity to bless someone who had blessed her every day before and after work. She told me she said a quick prayer while riding the bus home that day that if she saw the man again she would bless him. Well, the next day he was right there in front of her job where he usually was. She gave him $25.00 and told him "God bless you." She said he looked confused. As she turned to walk away, God told her to give him an additional $25.00; so she did.   She told me that he gave her something that was priceless every day: "a blessing." She said she felt the need to return the favor since she was fortunate to have a job, home and food on her table. Even though she had her own issues, her act of giving may have changed someone's life.

Advice: Do something for someone that you don't know. Give and receive a priceless blessing.

Set the Bar High

<u>**DAY 6**</u>

Setting the bar high means achieving a feat which will be difficult for others to reach and accomplish. When we set the bar high for ourselves we expect the best out of ourselves because we know our potential. It's good to set standards. When we do this it gives us something to look forward to. Self-discipline starts with acknowledging the need to draw a line in your life. Are you over indulging in food, sex, drugs, aggressive behavior or excessively spending money? Is this an issue which has gotten so far out of hand that you've lost someone close to you? Has this changed your outer appearance? Has it changed your thinking pattern?

In 2012, I used to indulge in drugs such as weed, pills and I even drank medicated cough syrup. One day I woke up and told myself I was tired. I was 32 years old, incarcerated and had a lot of time on my hands. I felt it was time to grow up and become a man. The same habits that landed me in prison were the same things I was continuing to indulge in. I challenged myself; I looked in the mirror and made a promise to myself I would never inhale another blunt or joint; I wouldn't use another drug not prescribed to me; and I would not pop another pill. I stuck to that promise.

Was it easy? Definitely not. I had the urge to just get away and use whatever crutch was available. But not only did I promise myself, I also set the bar high by telling my peers that I was no longer using any drug of any sort. I knew they would hold me to that. It's now 2015 and I haven't used. Period. Sometimes we must make promises to ourselves that we don't want to make but need to make. Then we must ask those close to us to hold us to those promises whether it's eating snacks, drinking alcohol, gambling, or spending money. Set the bar high!

Advice: When you make a promise to yourself, you have to keep it real with you!

Being Thankful For the Small Things

DAY 7

What are some of the first things that come to your mind when faced with the question, "What are you thankful for?" Is it your mother, job, kids, health, or some material possession? Whatever your answer may be, the question helps you to reflect on the things which you feel the need to show thanks and gratitude towards. Sometimes we tend to overlook the small things which are removed from our lives, or a situation where the small things play a big role in our lives, in order to realize the major impact those things have on our everyday lives. For example, right now many states are experiencing a water drought. California is one of the most populated states in America and water is something that is used to produce not only vegetation but to supply many businesses who in return supply the nation.

How many times have we taken something as simple as water for granted? Was this one of the things you were thankful for? When you shower or wash dishes do you keep track of your water consumption? Probably not. This may be due to your belief that water is everlasting. You know that when you turn the knob on a faucet, water will disperse. How would you feel if one day you turned the knob and nothing came out? Or the water was so filthy it was unusable? We need to see the things, people and positions we hold in life as being just as valuable as water and not abuse or misuse them. One day you may have everything and the next day you may have nothing or limited resources. Don't take things or people in your life—who you feel are small or irrelevant—for granted. You never know when you just might need them!

Advice: Take notice of the things or people you take for granted.

Do You Know Your Kids?

<u>**DAY 8**</u>

Kids. You've got to love them no matter how frustrated they make you. Sometimes our kids have the tendency to do things purposely just to get our attention. When was the last time you asked your kids what they liked, or what was going on in their lives? Try asking them and you'll be amazed at the answers you receive. It doesn't hurt to take one day out of the week to sit down with your kid for a full day and just learn things about them; asking questions you usually wouldn't ask them. As parents we all think we know our children. However, as soon as someone questions us about our child's character we jump on the defense, probably saying, "Oh no, my child wouldn't do that. They know better." But do they? Or do we just assume they know better? Some kids do know better and they act-out to get our attention. They may feel the need to do something awkward just so we can chastise them to show we care.

I had a familiar incident with my daughter. She had a younger sister half-sister) in the household who wasn't my biological daughter. I gave them both the same attention but I didn't know my daughter didn't like this. One day someone poured a new can of powdered baby milk all over the bedroom floor. My daughter's mother instantly blamed the younger daughter. The younger daughter kept saying, "Daddy Phillip it wasn't me, it was her," referring to my daughter. My daughter's mother yelled, "No, it wasn't! She's older and she knows better." When we found my daughter, she had powdered milk all over her! She cried and explained she didn't like her younger sister calling me "daddy," This was her way of getting her stepsister in trouble and getting my attention. Even though she was punished, I sat her down and explained that no one would ever take her place. She was my only princess!

Advice: Get to know your kids while they're young. They grow up fast!

Don't Waste Your Energy

<u>**DAY 9**</u>

What are you putting your energy into? Is it something constructive? Is it something which will benefit you in the long run? Is it a righteous cause? We need to be careful not to give our time and energy to the wrong things, especially if they don't bear good fruits or hurt others. I've been faced with adversity many times in my life. Whenever I applied negative energy to my adversity that is what I got in return: negativity. But whenever I tried to use positive energy to change the outcome of my situation or feelings, not only did I feel better but the results were much better. Sometimes we find ourselves entertaining things, people and situations that are not even worthy of our attention. After this is done we often find ourselves exhausted, frustrated and confused. Sometimes it's best to just stay positive no matter what the situation is. The energy alone is powerful enough to shift the direction of any circumstance you find yourself in.

There's been many times where I've been faced with verbal confrontations which could have turned into physical altercations. But by shifting the negative energy I had built up into positive energy, I was able to change the direction of the confrontation and avoid using negative energy to resolve a situation. Prayer and faith, along with works, is a mighty ingredient to use when faced with negative energy.   But sprinkle a little positive thinking and positive energy in there and you've got a recipe that will fulfill anyone's appetite no matter how negative it is! It's always good to have a positive attitude when going into any situation.   Your energy has the power to affect people for better or worse. How will you use your energy today?

**Advice: Positive energy can pump life into anything —
even negativity!**

Who Am I?

<u>DAY 10</u>

How we define ourselves is very important to the character we represent within ourselves. "Who am I?" is a question we may find we ask ourselves at least once in our lifetime. Well, who are you? Are you a leader? Are you a gifted musician? Are you a positive role model? Are you a wonderful parent? Are you a smart, intelligent and outstanding person? Who are you? What values and morals do you stand by in life? What are your fears? What are your likes and dislikes? Anytime I enter into a new relationship or meet new friends, before we proceed no further than introducing ourselves, I open the door to who I am. I inform them of my flaws, my likes, my dislikes and the morals I stand on in life. I've found this to be very responsible.

Too many times we jump into commitments without reading the fine print, knowing what we are getting ourselves into. If you are straight-forward with someone from the beginning, there are no strings attached and no surprises. Not only do you give others the opportunity to decline building a relationship with you, but you also open a door of comfort for them to tell you who they are and some interesting things about themselves they may feel are important for you to know. I remember I rushed into a relationship with a woman a few years ago. At that time we had never slept together or even gone out on a date. After months of talking on the phone, we decided to move in with each other. Big mistake! She didn't know I snored as loud as I did. It was so irritating to her she couldn't sleep and was tired the next day when it was time to go to work. Our relationship ended on that note. I'm sure there were other factors why we separated but the sleeping issue is what broke the ice. Had she known about my sleep apnea in the beginning she could have made the decision not to live together and still remained a friend. Lesson learned!

Advice: Put it all on the table from the beginning. Therefore, when it's time to enjoy dinner you don't spoil someone else's appetite!

Know Your Limitations

DAY 11

Sometimes we have the tendency to overcommit to people, schedules and even ourselves. When we find ourselves in uncomfortable situations due to these commitments, we sometimes tell ourselves, "I'm never doing that again." It's very important that we know our limitations. I consider myself a multi-tasker. I'm currently enrolled in college, I'm a G.E.D. tutor, I'm enrolled in several self-help classes, and I have several business projects I'm currently working on. Most of these tasks have deadlines which must be met. Due to my status and reputation for being business orientated, a lot of people ask for my assistance, whether it's putting together a business proposal, helping them prepare for a final exam, or looking over a business outline. Without thinking of my own priorities I commit myself to helping them. By the time I realize what I've done I'm drowned in work which I blindly committed to do. This frustrates me because I find myself asking, "Why didn't I just say no?"

It's not that easy. When you are a people-person and you deal with a lot of people on a day-to-day basis, you will sometimes find yourself agreeing to some term or commitment with these people. Through years of experience and learning the hard way, I've found it easier to tell people who need your assistance, "I'll see what I can do. I can't make any promises so let me get back to you." It's responsible and very professional. When dealing with our own time management and schedule, know your limitations and breaking point. Give yourself and your mind a rest period. Take a break and focus on finishing the task you have before you rather than jumping into one task after another. It's okay to multi-task but don't burn yourself out. It's also wise to have a strict schedule that you abide by. Exercise self-discipline.

Advice: If you can't do it just say you can't. You'll feel better the next day.

Tick, Tick, BOOM! — Self-Destruction

<u>DAY 12</u>

Do you have a fuse on you which is just waiting to be lit? Have you ever heard the expression "you're just a time bomb waiting to explode?" This statement is usually true for individuals who have anger issues or often find themselves in altercations more than usual. Do you have any built up anger or stress that you have yet to address and deal with? It's a good first step to acknowledge that you do have issues. Being in denial only makes things worse. For many years I thought that anger was bad and abnormal. I would do my best to try to hide it. Sometimes I had to smile when I really didn't want to for fear of being labeled "an angry person." Later on in life I learned—through a friend of mine who is counselor—that anger is normal. You have the right to be upset, mad and frustrated. It's what you do with anger that is considered abnormal.

But, what do you do when you have these feelings? Do you act-out by hurting yourself and others? Do you break things? Do you say and do hurtful things? How do you vent? It's wise to talk to someone you trust about issues you are dealing with in life whether present or past issues. When you do this, you give your emotions relief. Fresh air. You can try writing down your frustrations in a letter to yourself or the person you are upset with.

I've done this many times and found myself writing over 10 pages of frustrations down; wasting paper and ink, but not wasting energy; hurting myself or others because eventually I read the letter to myself. I calmed down, took a deep breath, ripped the letter up and threw it away. This worked for me. You may want to find something that works for you. You'll be amazed at how good you feel afterwards.

Advice: For every action there is a reaction; for every reaction there is a

consequence.   Control your anger, don't let your anger control you.

Are You Conceited or Confident?

<u>DAY 13</u>

Everyone wants to feel as if they are someone special in their own mind. I know I enjoy the feeling of putting on a nice pair of shoes, new shirt and pants and looking at myself in the mirror before I step out.   Once I do step out, I walk with confidence: head held high and a glow about me. Many people have told me this and that I have a presence that demands attention. Others have told me that I'm conceited. I recall a time when I'd gone to work like I do on any given day, smiling and greeting my co-workers, making small talk about a sporting game which took place the day before. My supervisor asked to see my files which held the work assignments for many of the students I was tutoring. While she looked through the files of the work my students completed, she asked to see their journals which held their writing assignments. I began to smile because since giving my students the journals I'd come up with some good topics for them to write about. As she opened one student's journal I chimed in with, "See, when I give them topics they like them so much they write two to three page journal entries." As I sat there smiling my supervisor erupted, responding, "You need to get off your high horse!"

Previously that week she had made a statement about me being conceited and too proud. So I responded by saying, "I will never get off my 'high horse' as you call it. I've been through a lot in my life and feel confident in my work performance and myself." Sometimes our confidence can offend people who don't know our story or the struggles we've experienced in life. As long as you don't intentionally put people down or attempt to make others feel small, it's okay to be confident and proud of your accomplishments. Give credit where it is due, even if it's to yourself!

Advice: Keep an umbrella. Someone may want to rain on your parade!

Humble Yourself During Adversity

<u>**DAY 14**</u>

The key to accepting things you cannot change is the power of humbleness. When you humble yourself, you're not giving in or tapping out. You are using your energy in a positive way to remain content with whatever is taking place in your life. A humble person shows good character traits. They will more than likely go out of their way to help others and avoid confrontation. With humbleness comes patience. When people see me in person, the first thing they probably notice is my size. Then if they are very observant they may notice my tattoos. If asked a question, when I do speak, they will notice my teeth are gold. They may assume I'm a street thug until they hold a conversation with me. Many will almost be shocked to see that I'm a humble individual who value the opinions of others and is very open minded.

Being a positive role model takes humbleness. You must learn to listen, look at both sides of the coin and open to constructive criticism. It's also good to humble yourself in the presence of other great people with the same, if not better, attributes than you. Sometimes our competitive nature wants others to know "I've already done that" or "I can do that, too; it's nothing." But when you humble yourself during challenges you find out who others are and more about yourself. Try to humble

The New Willie Lynch   Concrete Walls & Steel Bars
Mr. P. D. White

yourself in difficult situations and watch the outcome. Don't always be so quick to speak; learn to listen more. Instead of putting your foot down during adversity or conflict, try raising your level of consciousness and displaying more maturity. The skill of humbleness will take you further in life than a balloon full of arrogant pride.

Advice: Show humbleness when your character is at stake.

Compassion for Others Is Important

<u>**DAY 15**</u>

Life can make some of the nicest people very mean or even cold-hearted. Through trials and tribulations it's easy to pick up bad habits such as not caring for others when they are down and out or going through something because you didn't receive the benefit of the doubt when you were going through a stressful time in your life. I've ran through many hurdles in life which I couldn't jump over alone. Sometimes there was no one there to help me get over that hurdle either. So I just sat there looking at it until I figured out how to get over it. Once I did get over it I felt good. The good feeling was because the experience gave me more humbleness and compassion for others who may be running the race of their lives and get stopped by a hurdle which appears out of nowhere: the loss of a job, marital issues, health issues, money problems. You cannot sit back and act as if it's not their problem.

Anytime you see another human being suffering you must have enough compassion to at least offer some type of helping hand. I'm not recommending you go out and save the world, but when faced with the reality of someone in your presence that is clearly suffering, it's always good to have a little compassion and not just shrug your shoulders and turn a blind eye. Even if you think you got through your adversity alone, believe me, you didn't. There was a higher power larger than you involved. You didn't just get to the top on your own. You are not perfect to the point where you never have issues. Remember, the same things you went through yesterday, someone may be going through them today.

Advice: Before you judge how someone else walk, put on their shoes.

Understanding Life and It's Circumstances
<u>DAY 16</u>

Sometimes, in order for me to move past a rare circumstance that I don't understand, I need closure. It's not enough to just let it pass. I must investigate the who, how, when and why of the situation. When I don't get the answers I'm looking for I become more frustrated than I was about the original issue. This has taught me to just except things for what they are and not to try so hard to figure out the "why" of everything I go through in life. Humans tend to do this: Why did my relationship end? Why did I get cut off in traffic? Why didn't someone answer the phone? Why did I get passed up for a promotion at work? Sometimes that's just life. There is no conspiracy against you. No one is out to embarrass you or purposely insult you. And even if the latter is true, you don't owe the situation so much attention that you neglect your daily duties and priorities.

Move forward with your life; get over it. Things happen which we don't need to know every answer to. Sometimes it's best we don't know the true reason behind other's motives because it can have an adverse effect on our way of thinking. I've learned that the true people in my life who care about me will be adults and reveal their motives for doing whatever it is that they did. And for those who don't, it's not my job to waste my energy trying to figure out the why, when, what and how. I could put that time into other important things like my career, children and health. Realize you are in control of your destiny. Don't give your power to something or someone to the level where they could dictate how you use your time. Be wise enough to accept things just for what they are — Things!

Advice: Move forward and don't waste time trying to figure out what's going on   behind you.

Believe In Yourself and You Won't Need Anyone Else To

DAY 17

Motivation. We all love a little motivation whether it comes from our mothers, fathers, spouses, loved ones or friends. Even our "haters" can motivate us if they hate on us enough. But with motivation comes believing that you can complete a task or reach a goal. Do you have self-motivation? Do you have self-confidence? Do you believe in yourself? Believing in you means entering into a situation or challenge with a positive attitude which says, "I can do this." Once you believe in yourself and your own accomplishments you really don't need anyone else to do so. Although it will still feel good to have a few supporters rooting for you, it really won't matter because you've built up the inner-belief that you've got this, you can do this and you will conquer whatever it is that needs to be conquered.

Sometimes we have the tendency to knock ourselves out of the fight before the bell even rings. We get in the ring and encounter an obstacle and before we even attempt to try we'll say, "I can't do this" or "This is too hard" or "I know I'll fail. I always do." We take ourselves out of the competition and give victory to the opponent. Remember, you are your own worst enemy and biggest and worst opponent! Try looking in the mirror sometimes and realize that the image you see in front of you is also your challenger. Are you that intimidating? No matter how big the mountain before you appears, if you continue to strike at it eventually it'll fold. You may hit it 99 times and just when you think it's not going to give in, you strike it that 100th time and it crumbles! Don't quit. Tell yourself, "I can do this!"

Advice: Half of the fight is your belief that you can walk away with a victory!

Be Honest With Yourself

<u>DAY 18</u>

I think it would be very beneficial for each human being to start looking in the mirror when they promise themselves something. By doing this, you put pressure on your conscience to be honest with yourself. However, that's only one useful exercise you can apply to your life if you seriously want to commit to something important in your life. We must learn to start being real with ourselves before we can be real with others. I remember one time I told myself I would stop eating too many sweets. At the time I made this promise to myself I was slightly overweight and at risk for high blood pressure.   But as soon as the opportunity presented itself for me to purchase a lot of sweets, I began to lie to myself and say, "I'll just eat one here and one there and save the rest. It will be easy." That was a lie. Eventually I ate all the sweets I purchased in a week's time.

Afterwards I felt bad, not because I ate the sweets so quickly, but because I lied to myself. I pumped myself up to believe I wouldn't be tempted to overindulge in a bad habit. It's always good to set limitations which we can live with and adjust to meet our intended goals. Instead of trying to commit to the impossible, set a small goal. Instead of buying a week's worth of sweets, I simply could have purchased two days of sweets. Just knowing something is limited will make us slow down and save it so you don't feel as guilty if you didn't achieve the goal you set. You can apply this to spending habits, going out, eating out, using the internet, using profanity, etc.   Instead of setting unrealistic goals, try setting goals that are achievable. You can also remove yourself from situations which may cause you to break your promise to yourself.

Advice: Know yourself, know your limitations. You set the bar!

Push Forward...Get Out the Rearview Mirror
<u>DAY 19</u>

Do you tend to stare at life through a rearview mirror? That is, are you one of those people who stay stuck so long in the past that it's hard to move forward? *Attachment.* We all get attached to things, people and places. But when those things, people and places have run their courses it's time to let them go. My grandmother once told me, "Grandson, life has chapters and you have people, places and things in those chapters of life. When it's time for the chapter to end it must end. Some chapters may be longer than others, but they eventually must end. You must learn to let them go, to move on and to say GOODBYE. That's *GOOD-BYE!*

Pushing forward is somewhat of a hard task for many of us who get attached to things easily and don't know how to let go. You must not become so obsessed with people, places and things that you can't accept losing them or moving forward. When the chapter ends you will find yourself hurt, feeling scorned and trying to back-pedal to recover something that's already over. Pushing forward can mean finding new things which await you in the future. It's that ol' saying, "If you continue to hold onto that dollar bill in your hand, you can't receive the hundred dollar bill which God has for you." Let go. Allow God to work in your life. If you quit trying to drive your own car, you're liable to wreck it. Sit behind the wheel and allow God to drive. Instead of cruise control, call it "God-control." There's more to life than what we see on a day-to-day basis. This is just a glimpse. I used to tell my friends in the neighborhood, "Man, get out and see the world. You act like you're going to miss something if you leave the hood for a few days." Grow, elevate, evolve, bloom, expand and move forward!

Advice: Don't stay stuck at the point where the rainbow starts. Find out where it ends. There may be a pot of gold awaiting you.

You Own Your Self-Esteem

DAY 20

Have you ever met someone that *you* feel has low self-esteem? What was your judgment based upon? Was it their appearance? How they responded to life? Or, was it because they were loners? How do you rate your self-esteem? Would you say it's moderate? Whatever your answer may be remember, self-esteem is yours. We are quick to point out that many people display low self-esteem. But to them they may feel they're doing just fine and have higher self-esteem than the person analyzing them. I once brought up the discussion of self-esteem to an African-American woman I worked with. When I made a comment about people having low self-esteem and needing a little encouragement from others, she didn't agree. In fact, what she said next made sense. She responded by saying, "Mr. White, if this is self-esteem, it's mine. I own it so who is the judge of how I use it?" Her response made me see things from a different perspective.

Although I believe you can tell when people around you are going through things and are suffering emotionally and mentally, it is hard to judge a person's self-esteem. What we may feel is normal self-esteem may be looked at as having low self-esteem. For example, I've met people who can appear to have it all together: the look, walk, talk, material things and money. From the outside looking in you could say this person has high or good self-esteem just based on how they present themselves to the world. But it's also a proven fact that people can hide behind facades and appearances. Then on the other hand you may have someone the total opposite who dresses in bargain clothes, drives a bucket, hangs alone and doesn't keep up their appearance to our standards. You would probably say this person has low self-esteem, when in all actuality they may feel better than the person who has all the things listed above. Assumptions; we all make them!

Advice: Self-esteem is yours, you own it and you don't have to flaunt it!

Wisdom: It's The Key to Life

<u>**DAY 21**</u>

True wisdom involves not only intelligence but also moral integrity. God is the source of wisdom. Experience is a great teacher. Through experience you gain both knowledge and wisdom. Knowing things are not enough to live life. You must be wise enough to apply what you know to your life to move forward and become fruitful. Wisdom is priceless. Once you've found it you will have earned the great reward which life has to offer.

Wisdom also grows. A wise man will inherit more wisdom as he gets older; only a fool will deny wisdom which will cost him in the end. Throughout my life I try to gain as much knowledge as possible by listening to my elders, reading, observing the mistakes that others make and living my life. The life-lessons I do learn I'll be able to apply them to my life in the future in a positive way rather than in a self-destructive way. This is wisdom; when you can learn something and apply it to your life so that you don't make the same mistakes again.

Wisdom comes with age. Ever heard the old saying, "Live long enough and you'll see just what I'm talking about." Sometimes when we are having jewels dropped on us we have the tendency to say, "I already know that." Well, if you already know then why is there a need for you to be told over and over about the same mistakes you keep making? It's wise to just listen. Take what you can from the message and apply the important things you learned to your life if they are beneficial and apply to you. Don't be so naïve and foolish that "you know it all." Only a fool is wise in his own eyes. Through God, you'll find wisdom if you allow your car to ride on "God-control." Who knows, you might even grow some gray hair when you find true wisdom.

Advice: "Iron sharpens iron." God gave us two ears and one mouth. Be slow to speak and quick to listen. You've got two ears; use them. One mouth; save it!

Knowledge: Know It...Retain it...Use It

DAY 22

When we learn new things in life we enjoy the luxury of being able to share the things we've learned with others. I am blessed to have many friends. A majority of my friends are into sports, like I am. They can tell you all the recent stats, highlights on ESPN and the latest draft picks. I also found out that the only sections in the newspaper they read was either the section which detailed crime in their city or the sports section. It was as if these were the only interesting sections of the newspaper.

One day while discussing the NBA standings the newspaper had just released, I asked my friend to pass me the business section of the paper. He looked at me strangely and asked, "You really read that stuff, man?" I said, "Of course." So I gave him a scenario: What happens if you are out and about—let's say at a local sports bar—and while having a drink, a man sitting at the bar next to you ask you how you feel about things other than sports (economy, politics, etc.)? You look dumbfounded as he continues to ask you about Wall Street, the Dow Jones, shares, investments, the stock market, etc. You can't answer him adequately so the conversation ends and he goes about his business. But what if you had knowledge about those subjects and the two of you began to get into a deep conversation? And what if after that conversation he pulled out his business card in which showed he owned his own stock brokerage company, law firm or real estate company. You would have just opened a potential door of opportunity for you. It's always wise and beneficial to retain as much knowledge as possible. You never know when you will need it for future references.

Advice: Read and learn as much as you can about life because you may be tested one day. Be ready for a pop quiz!

Strength Within Is Powerful

<u>**DAY 23**</u>

Exercising daily does build up your muscles. It's healthy and relieves many people of stress. But when they say "only the strong survive" they don't mean go out and get a 24-hour fitness card, personal trainer and buff it out. No, strength of this sort comes from within, mentally and emotionally. Building this type of strength comes from trials and tribulations and experiencing adversity in our lives. When we encounter these tests in life not only do they build character but they build a brick wall that "no weapon formed against you" can penetrate.

I've had many letdowns in life: Broken promises by friends, family and girlfriends; dreams shattered from unexpected circumstances. My son was hit by a DUI (Driving Under the Influence) motorist and was almost killed. My step-daughter was diagnosed with ALL (a form of leukemia) and I lost my grandmother and uncle a year apart. These things caused me a lot of turmoil in life. It was hard to get over these events but through prayer and building an in-depth relationship between God and myself, I was able to get over these hurdles and continue on my journey.

What these situations did to my life and character was strengthen them. I knew that if I could get through life-changing events like these I could go through many things. I knew it didn't mean my experiences would be any easier to deal with because of this inner-strength, but I knew that I could survive. The devil has his way of getting into our minds and feeding on our strengths until we are weakened. He knows what makes us suffer and hurt and he knows what we rely on to get over that suffering. So he tries to attack from both ends. Continue to do mental pushups and sit-ups and you'll have the strength needed to fight him off when he does arrive. God is also the best resource as a personal trainer!

Advice: With God as your personal trainer and life as your treadmill, you'll be ready to run a marathon!

Concrete Walls & Steel Bars — Break The Chains!
DAY 24

Good morning, good evening, good life. How are you feeling? Incarceration isn't just a physical reality it's also a mental and emotional state that many of us find ourselves in. Do you find yourself shackled and confined to the trash which you've allowed to pile up inside of your mind? Our minds are really like cells. You have walls and bars which keep things in and out, but they can sometimes let in small things which can become detrimental to our progress. You have doors with lock and keys which sometimes keep us secluded from the real world and reality. How does your cell look? Do you allow your cell to define you or do you define the cell? Is the bed made up in your cell where you rest peacefully or is it unmade, covers everywhere like a permanent resting place for you to drown in your misery while you do time there for life? Who do you allow in your cell while you're doing your time? What do you allow in your cell as you carry out your sentence? In your spare time what goes on in your cell? How does it look? How does it smell?   Is it pleasant or corroded with nasty, poisonous things?

When we think about our mind we can compare it to a cell. A cell doesn't necessarily have to be a jail cell either; just a space reserved for you to take a vacation from everything. How you

196

perceive the cell is how it will appear. If you look at it as being doom, gloomy, depressing and something you'd rather not deal with, then that's what it will be. You are as you think. If you allow negative pictures to be hung on the wall in your cell, then eventually those are the same pictures you will see and view everyday of your life until you decide to tear them down. If you allow bad memories to stay in your suitcase under your bed, then they will remain there, tormenting you until you decide to clean out your cell. You can't just sweep things under the rug. You must sweep the negative things into a pile, place them on a dustpan and throw them out of your life for good!

And don't allow someone else's cell to become your cell, too. Be careful who you allow in your cell. People can bring their excess luggage to your cell and corrupt it with things that your cell is not built to withstand. If you must live in that cell of yours you might as well keep it clean. "You can lock me up physically, but mentally I'm free!" Always remember that quote no matter where you are in life. You can be committed to a job, career, relationship, hobby or a variety of things. However, you don't have to be confined to them to the point where you can't have your own time of solitude and space. Life is meant to have ups and downs, smiles and frowns. Just remember, you don't have to let those things be the chapter in your life that ends before it even gets started. Dirt and dust will find its way into your cell, but you must do a thorough job of constantly cleaning and dusting it out to rid it of any foreign dirt, dust and objects.

Let your cell be a peaceful platform; somewhere you can go when things seem as if they are too hard to allow you to move forward. Let your cell become your rest haven! You should be able to resort to your willpower and inner strength when faced with adversity. Your mind needs that free space which you can move around in when you need to be mobile. Many people have their minds so full of clutter and distraction that they don't know where to begin. They can't think properly because there's too much in the way of their thinking. Try readjusting your thinking habits. Try building barriers in your mind which negativity cannot penetrate. Take inventory on what is being brought into your mind. Is it an asset or liability? Does it have the potential to be destructive in the future? Does it alter your perception on life as a whole? Do you like it?

We must be very careful what we feed our minds. Just as the mind is like a cell, it can also be compared to a child who is always learning new things; still in the molding process. Even as adults our minds must be treated like that of a child, meaning you have to be careful of the things you say to it, give to it and show it because the mind stores those things for later use. Treat your mind like a garden: plant positive seeds in it, water it, feed it and nurture it properly and those positive seeds will blossom into a beautiful sight to see. For those of you who have grown up around negativity and poisonous environments, don't allow those things to define who you are today. Don't allow your mind to be a reflection of those things.

Break the chains and release yourself from your mental incarceration. Life has a way of holding us by the wrists and ankles and not allowing us to become mentally mobile. Stress enters into that stage of our lives where we feel exhausted and at times we just don't have enough energy to fight it off. It's okay. Stressing a little is not abnormal. It's perfectly normal and we all do it. But after you have stressed, it's time to move forward. Dust yourself off and be thankful that you are still breathing no matter what the circumstances are.

The media is a negative resource at times. It has a lot of control over our minds and the way we think. They can take a situation, put a twist on it and breathe negativity into the minds of vulnerable people. The internet has the power to pollute the mind with trash and negativity. It's so easy to be on Facebook chatting when something pops up on your screen and takes your attention off of what you were doing, or someone else's blog or statements have an adverse effect on you.

The music we listen to has its way of altering our minds and how we perceive things, people and places. If your choice of music is rap, and a rapper is telling you how prejudiced a particular city is, nine times out of ten your mind registers that information and uses it in the future. So now when you visit this particular city you are already on guard just based off of what you heard. We must be very careful of what we allow our minds to separate the difference between what is real, fiction, opinions, controversy, conspiracies and reliable resources.

The people we associate with on a day-to-day basis have the most impact on our lives and our minds. Your circle and choice of friends are considered a reflection of you. It's been said that, "People who want to get rich hang with rich folks, dope fiends hang with dope fiends, criminals hang with criminals and so on." This is not proven to be 100% factual, but it does hold its own weight in the society we live in today. Negativity is glorified so much nowadays that if you aren't a part of the negative energy you may be looked at as an off brand outsider. A lot of this has to do with the way people minds are programmed and what they perceive to be "righteous" or cool.

Being in the in-crowd has its disadvantages. Believe me, I know. Sometimes we will go against the grain of our own morals and beliefs in order to be accepted. I'm sure we've all encountered one or two of these experiences in life. It's normal. As kids we do it, as adolescents we do it and as adults we do it. That gut feeling will tell you it's not right; your wisdom and knowledge will be there to assure you it's not right; and your conscience (mind) will slap you and tell you it's totally against what you stand for, but you do it anyway. If the consequences outweigh the reward, you can either remove that thought process out of your mind or choose to keep it and continue to suffer in the ocean of life surrounded by your own mental sharks.

In order to break the chains which have our minds confined to one-track programming we must want to use the keys provided to us. It's good to have people around you that you trust to give you good advice when you are faced with life-altering options. It's also good to have people around you who tell you what you need to hear versus what you want to hear. Anytime you find someone who is willing to use their supply of oxygen to give you good advice or tell you where you are making mistakes in your life, you've found a friend. It's easy to find "yes men" and "yes women" who agree with any and every idea we have. But when you find a genuine person who doesn't benefit at all from what they are telling you and only want to see you succeed in life, you've found a rare jewel. Everyone is not out to get you or run your life or dictate your "program." Some people love you enough to tell you the truth! Those people are really hard to find so when you find one keep them. It's like a diamond in the dirt: you never know what it is until you pick it up and examine it a little closer.

Advice: Take inventory of the things in your mind. Are you hoarding unnecessary trash which is polluting your train of thought?

Part 3

The Third and Final Door to Reprogramming Your Mind

CHAPTER 8

THE 7 CONTRACTS YOU WILL SIGN THAT WILL CHANGE YOUR LIFE FOREVER

Congratulations

Congratulations! You have just completed the first 24 days of reprogramming your mind. How do you feel? You should feel extremely proud of yourself if you've made it this far. What new things did you learn about yourself? Did you spot any unnoticed flaws which you need to work on? How many new relationships did you build with family and friends? Are you on the right track with your children? Have you pinpointed what causes you to get sidetracked in life? Over the next 7 days you will deal with the hardest part of the 31-day reprogramming of your mind. This section of the book holds the key to breaking the chains off of your thought process, moving forward and being honest with yourself.

Have you ever signed a contract in your life? If you've been following along in the book you may have signed one earlier in Chapter 2. The next 7 days hold the contracts to your life. You can tear these contracts out of the book, copy them or keep them in the book. If you decide to pass the book along for a friend to read, they'll see the commitment you've made to change and may want to make the same commitment. Whatever you decide to do with the contracts, they're yours. You can leave them blank if you feel you're not yet fully prepared to commit to change. The purpose of the contract is to build up that drive in you to move forward. It's a little reminder that you've made a promise with yourself. If you can sign a lease and keep it you should be able to sign a contract with promises you made to yourself and keep these promises.

Give yourself a chance. Take it one day at a time. You are the manager of your life; the landlord who controls the lease. Therefore, how you accept payment based on stipulations in your contract is on you and you alone. No one is forcing you to sign these contracts. You are not being held against your will when signing these contracts. You have the option of not even looking at the contracts. But until you take that first step forward in reprogramming your thoughts about how you see yourself and others and how you view life, you will have a long journey ahead of you.

If you have access to a copy machine it's helpful to copy each contract and hang them up where you can see them. If you have access to a scanner it would be beneficial to upload the contracts to your internet page and challenge family and friends to join you in the 31-day reprogramming of the mind exercise. Get involved with your spouse when you sign these contracts and ask them to hold you to your end of the deal. Get involved with your children and let them know you are trying something new and would like them to assist you. Tell a friend or co-worker and encourage them to try it out. What do you have to lose?

Can you resist your desire to stay stagnated in neutral, doing the same things which have gotten you the same results year in and year out? Well, here's your opportunity. You are not alone. I'm reprogramming with you and the only difference is that I'm on a lifetime reprogramming of the mind. You, too, can do this. What's the recipe? Just reading the first 24 days one exercise each day and reviewing the contracts you signed for the last 7 days. The contracts are the personal trainer who's behind you pushing you when you feel as if you can't keep up. The contracts are you, telling yourself, "I got your back, don't give up, we're almost there!" These contracts are mirror images of you and your desire to change! Good luck!

The contracts I've prepared consist of By Laws which apply to self — YOU! The contracts were drawn up based on previous reprogramming skills that you learned throughout the last chapter. Out of the 24 days you've already completed, 7 of those days were based solely on you and reprogramming of the self. The 7 contracts include:

Day #25 — This contract is based on Day #10 "Who Am I"

Day #26 — This contract is based on Day #11 "Know Your Limitations"

Day #27 — This contract is based on Day #12 "Self-Destruction"

Day #28 — This contract is based on Day #14 "Humble Yourself Through Adversity"

Day #29 — This contract is based on Day #17 "Believing In Self"

Day #30 — This contract is based on Day #18 "Being Honest to Self"

Day #31 — This contract is based on Day #20 "You Own Your Self-Esteem"

These days were selected based on the need for you to get closer to who you are as a person. These contracts will help you mold yourself into the "true you" if you stick to the guidelines and remain focused. It won't be enough to just sign the contracts, you should want to live the contracts. Have a positive outlook entering into the contract and you'll have the same positive attitude once you fulfill the stipulations in the contract. You hold the key. Are you ready to unlock the chains?

Reprogramming Of The Mind Contract of Agreement

DAY 25

Agreement, entered into as of this _____ day of _____, 20___.

I, _____, have willfully signed this contract pertaining to "Who Am I." I understand that in order for me to move forward in life and become all that I am created to be, I need to know "Who I Am." I am: _____, _____,_____, and _____, a person who has goals and ambitions in life. These goals consist of: _____

_____

I understand I have flaws. I am only human. I do not expect to be perfect. I am content knowing I am not perfect and I'm continuing to work on the flaws I have, which consist of:

_____

_____

I intend to work on these flaws as of _____, day of _____, 20 _____. I love myself. I understand that change is a process and every process has needs that must be met. By signing this contract I agree to be true to myself and respect myself, be happy with who I am and live my life to the fullest, not concerned about what others think of me. I now love myself enough to know "Who I am" so that I never have to ask myself again, "Who Am I."

By placing my initials here _____ I am in agreement that I understand what I am signing and agreeing to.

X_____

Date _____

(Signature)

Reprogramming Of The Mind Contract of Agreement

DAY 26

Agreement, entered into as of this _____ day of _____, 20___ .

I, _____, have willfully signed this contract pertaining to "Knowing my Limitations." I understand that in order for me to move forward in life and become all that I am created to be I need to *know my limitations*. I am aware that in order for me to identify my limitations I must know them, respect them, control them and not allow them to control me. I must not allow my commitment to things I have no ultimate control over to dictate my commitment I have to myself to be at peace in life. The limitations which I am setting as of ____, day of ____, 20 ___ are:

_____

_____

I understand these limitations must be set. In the past, I have committed to people and tasks that I was not prepared to commit to. Today I am setting guidelines and limitations. In order for me to abide by the limitations I have set for myself, I will:

_____

_____

I will not feel guilty. This doesn't mean I don't love helping others or pursuing my career, hopes or dreams, it just mean that I know my boundaries and limitations and I am now taking control of the things which have taken control over my life for so long. In order for me to fulfill my commitments and be a responsible person, I need to "Know my Limitations."

By placing my initials here _____ I am in agreement, that I understand what I am signing and agreeing to.

X_____

Date _____

(Signature)

Reprogramming Of The Mind Contract of Agreement

DAY 27

Agreement, entered into as of this _____ day of _____,20_____.

I, _____, have willfully signed this contract pertaining to "Self-Destruction." I understand that in order for me to avoid *self-destruction* I must know what sets me off, sparks my fuse and triggers a negative response from me. As of now I am identifying with several of my self-destructive ways which include, but are not limited to: _____

_____

_____

I understand I have triggers. I am working on those triggers. I do not expect to change overnight. I'm content knowing I am not perfect and I'm continuing to work on those triggers I have which consist of: _____

_____

I have taken the first step to admitting I have self-destructive ways which are very detrimental to me and others around me. The triggers that set me off must be addressed and dealt with accordingly in order for the process of growth and development to take effect. In order for me to prevent my own self-destruction I am agreeing on this _____, day of _____, 20____that I will:

_____

_____

In order to diffuse any anger, frustration, unwarranted stress that builds up in me, I can no longer _____ because these things go against what I stand for and what I am trying to achieve in life. If I do find myself in a stressful, confrontational situation I will: _____

_____

I understand that anger is normal. It is what I do with anger that can be considered abnormal. It takes only a second to make a mistake and a lifetime to correct one.

By placing my initials here _____ I am in agreement that I understand what I am signing and agreeing to.

X _____

Date _____

(Signature)

Reprogramming Of The Mind Contract of Agreement

DAY 28

Agreement, entered into as of this _____ day of _____, 20_____.

I, _____, have willfully signed this contract pertaining to "Humbling Myself During Adversity." I understand that in order for me to *humble myself during adversity* I must learn to accept things that I cannot change. I must set my pride aside and display the characteristics of a mature and humble individual. I can become more humble when:

_____

_____

I now know that with humbleness comes patience. As of _____, day of _____, 20_____, I will begin to show my humbleness by:

_____

_____

_____

I am working hard at learning myself and how I react and respond around others when my character is in question. I know who I am. I do not need to always have the last word, know it all, debate or become argumentative. I'm content with humbly folding my hands, knowing that I am a more humble person who can move forward in life. This does not mean I bowed out or tapped out or gave up. It means I have grown up! Not every challenge needs a challenger.

By placing my initials here _____ I am in agreement that I understand what I am signing and agreeing to.

X _____

Date _____

(Signature)

Reprogramming Of The Mind Contract of Agreement

DAY 29

Agreement, entered into as of this _____ day of _____, 20_____.

I, _____, have willfully signed this contract pertaining to "Believing In Self." I understand that in order for me to *believe in myself* I must continue to display self-confidence and not question my ability to prosper. I must go into my daily challenges knowing that they will be hard but with effort, I can overcome any obstacle. My strength is my strength and I will continue to build it up as I journey through and learn new things about life and myself. There will be times when I may feel exhausted but I know that I must continue to push forward and strive for greatness. I can begin this process by believing in myself more when it comes to:

_____

_____

As of _____, day of _____, 20 _____, I will begin my process into believing in myself more than I have in the past.

I understand I must wake up confident and go to sleep with even more confidence that today was a fruitful day and I did all that I could to see to it that I didn't give into negativity or defeat. When I believe in myself, I feel:

_____

_____

I enjoy this feeling. I have things that I want to accomplish in life which consist of: _____

_____

I believe that I can achieve these goals and overcome any obstacle in my journey along the way!

By placing my initials here _____ I am in agreement that I understand what I am signing and agreeing to.

X   _____

Date _____

(Signature)

Reprogramming Of The Mind Contract of Agreement

DAY 30

Agreement, entered into as of this _____ day of _____, 20____.

I, _____, have willfully signed this contract pertaining to "Being Honest to Self." I understand that in order for me to *be honest with myself* I must continue to realize that I have things in my life that I do need to work on. I cannot sweep these issues under the rug and act as if they do not exist. For years I have deceived others and myself by not being completely honest about who I am and what I am going through personally. I am now trying to gain control of my life but now understand that in order to finish this process I must be honest with me _____. When I look in the mirror, I see a _____ person.

When I think about myself, I think of :

_____

_____

The person I used to be is no longer around. Today I am:

_____

_____

Others around me can rest assured I will start being:

_____

_____

As of _____, day of _____, 20_____, I will begin my process of being honest with myself more than I have in the past.

Being honest with me means I must:

_____

I enjoy being honest with myself because:

_____

_____

I believe that I can be the "true me" and still love who I am regardless of my past mistakes and flaws.

By placing my initials here _____ I am in agreement that I understand what I am signing and agreeing to.

X _____

Date _____

(Signature)

Reprogramming Of The Mind Contract of Agreement

DAY 31

Agreement, entered into as of this _____ day of _____, 20____.

I, _____, have willfully signed this contract pertaining to "Owning My Self-Esteem." I understand that in order for me to *own my self-esteem* I must continue to realize that it doesn't matter how others see me. I feel good knowing I am who I am and what I'm not I can never be! My self-esteem belongs to me _____. My self-esteem is not on display for others to criticize. I do not have to go out of my way to prove my self-esteem to others. I do not have to sound the trumpet when I am feeling good or make a big announcement when I have accomplished a great feat. I can enjoy the moment with myself and those who genuinely care for me. In the past I may have had issues with my confidence, my outer appearance or my communication skills. However, I am only human and I am working every day at bettering myself. Some things which got me down in the past were:

_____

Now that I have identified these things I can work on them. Anything in my life which is a hindrance to my self-esteem must be removed immediately. It can no longer sit around and destroy me. I love to _____

I love myself because:_____

No one can take my pride, dignity or integrity from me anymore. No one will be able to succeed at putting me down and holding me down. I feel good. I love myself more than anything in life did.

As of _____, day of _____, 20_____ I will begin my process into "Owning My Self-Esteem" more than I have in the past.

Having my self-esteem to me means I must _____

I own my self-esteem. It's all mine!

By placing my initials here _____ I am in agreement that I understand what I am signing and agreeing to.

X _____

Date _____

(Signature)

Part 4

EXPERIENCE IS THE BEST TEACHER IN LIFE

CHAPTER 9

Learning From Your Pop Quizzes in Life

Life is the best teacher you can turn to if a lesson is needed for growth. Recently I interviewed a female friend of mine who had just gone through a very disruptive relationship. As she began to pour out her heart and the details, she constantly blamed herself. I stopped her and explained to her that, "As a woman, you did exactly what any real woman would do. You gave your man your all and it wasn't your fault he didn't return the same favor, loyalty and gratitude." She went on to tell me how in the beginning this man was so nice; came off very spiritual and respectful. Looking for love, she allowed him not only into her heart but her home where eventually she and her kids became prisoners. She said it was as if he changed right before her eyes. He started staying out late and taking her car; emptying her bank account and causing confusion with her and the kids; and tearing out her bank account plus tearing up her home.

After I asked several more personal questions I came to the conclusion that the man was on drugs and appeared to suffer from a severe mental illness. She corroborated my conclusion by telling me he informed her he was a veteran of war and had been diagnosed with PTSD. I could tell from how she poured out her heart to me that all she needed was a real friend. After having her bank account empty and car stolen, she eventually filed criminal charges against him. This crazy man had the nerve to call her collect from jail and ask, "Why you put me in jail?" She said her response was, "Fool, you put yourself in jail. Goodbye!"

Today this woman is stronger than ever. She gives me a lot of credit for her newly found strength but I take no credit at all. I told her, "Sister it was always inside of you. You just had to go through a life-altering situation to teach you some valuable lessons in life. You did nothing wrong at all other than love someone who truly never loved you." Women and men, you need to stop beating yourself up when you are faced with adversity. Look for the positive that's found in every negative. We have the tendency to blame ourselves when things don't go as planned. If your father wasn't in your life how is that your fault? If your husband cheated on you why blame yourself? If your wife divorced you and took the kids, why do you feel you are responsible? There are going to be things others do right before your eyes which are out of your control. It's time you start realizing this. You can't continue to punish yourself for every failure in life. Instead, look at the mistakes you've made, make some corrections and prepare yourself for the next pop quiz!

When moving forward in life, sometimes you can glance back just to see how far you've come. You can reminisce and think of the good and bad times which brought you to the point where you now rest. But don't ponder on the past too long. It's time to keep your eyes on the prize which awaits you in the future. What happened then, happened. It's over. We can't go back and correct it. But, we can rewrite history by never allowing the same things to happen again. Study life. Look over the wrong answers you got and be prepared to be retested. You'll be surprised when you score an A-plus on the next pop quiz!

CHAPTER 10

Your Journey Continues

Keep on pushing young brother and sister, keep on pushing. The journey you now walk may have deep thick gravel on the road along with large tree stumps and large, heavy stones blocking your pathway to the other side. However, if there is a will there is a way. The will is through God who provides a way. Your journey continues. It doesn't end because you got laid off at your job you've had for years. It doesn't stop because of a failed relationship or marriage. It's not over because you got wounded in war and lost a limb. No, the journey continues. Keep fighting for your right to live a happy, stress-free, carefree, peaceful and joyous life. You've earned that right. Don't bathe in your losses, sitting there counting them and trying to figure out how to regain your status. Instead, move forward and keep pushing because you never know what blessings await you at the other end of your journey. A journey has a starting point and an ending point. No matter how long it is, it has to start and it has to stop somewhere.

Now, the beginning of the journey may be hard but if you continue, you will probably have endured many trials and tribulations which will better prepare you for what awaits you up the road. Or, the beginning of your journey may be easy and you may not experience any turmoil until you get towards the end. However, you will still experience the adversity that you need to finalize your journey and build the character that will let you be able to say, "I've been there and done that." Never give the devil the glory of quitting. You've come too far to turn around now and throw it all away!

Some of us need a hard walk through life to prepare us for an even harder walk up the road. Those who go through life and never suffer, or go through trials and tribulations at some point, have it harder once they do experience the downfalls of life because they don't know how to deal with them. Take a child who has been fed with a "silver spoon" their entire life; how do they expect to survive if their life-line is finally cut off and they are forced to survive on their own with no support from family and friends? They will either lose their minds, commit suicide, turn to drug use, or become part of the small percentage who actually do take the adversity head on and deal with it. Some can't fathom the thought of mom and dad not taking care of them for the rest of their lives. The thought alone drives them crazy. So it's best to allow life to serve you now and you go through what is destined for you to go through. Therefore, you will be prepared in the future when disaster strikes again.

Those who have never been in a rainstorm will more than likely never purchase an umbrella until it's too late. But run into someone who's been caught in several rainstorms and experience has taught them to keep an umbrella in the house, car at work and anywhere else they may stop. But once we learn, we continue to move forward. Let's keep trying. We are almost at the finish line. It doesn't matter if you have to walk at a slow pace, crawl or electric slide to reach your goal, just don't quit. Keep on pushing and don't stop!

CHAPTER 11

The Key: The Chains Have Been Broken!

I present you with this key. It's yours to use if you feel as if you are ready to release those chains that have held you captive your entire life. Life has so much to offer if you keep your hands open and await the blessings God has prepared for you. Right now as this book is being published, crime is at an all-time high across the nation. Police shootings are higher than ever before. And when I say police shootings I mean "the police shooting!" But you cannot allow these unfortunate events to keep you hiding in the house of your own mind, stagnating and afraid to grow. Don't allow the negativity which goes on around you to pull you in. Keep moving. Be an asset to your community instead of a liability. Help solve the problems in your community and don't be the problem. Men be men and women be women. Mothers be mothers and fathers be fathers. Raise our young seeds to provide, protect and prosper. To each one teach one. Encourage your fellow brothers and sisters to educate themselves and learn as much as possible because education is the key. Stop hating one another and start loving one another. Stop pointing the finger and start accepting responsibility.

The New Willie Lynch   Concrete Walls & Steel Bars
Mr. P. D. White

It is true: we do reap what we sow. So let's start sowing some good seeds so our harvest can reap when it really counts. If you are someone in a position of power, please use that power wisely to change the lives of the people around you for the better. If you are fortunate and blessed to have a fortune, do something positive with it which will create opportunity for the community in which you live. Our society needs those old school boys and girls clubs, peewee football leagues and debate clubs. We need to encourage our children to enter more spelling bees and science fairs instead of just looking at iPhone screens and Facebook pages. There is a world outside of their home and how they choose to live in it is their choice. The children are the future and it is the duty of every adult to step up and be responsible for what we do in the presence of the future.

Our celebrity entertainers must be held accountable for their actions and what they put out there. Parents must start monitoring the things their children watch and listen to. It's time to be parents to our kids not their friends. It's time to put our foot down and not merely talk about what we want out of life but be what we want out of life. It's time to practice what we preach and not be hypocrites. It's time for pastors, ushers and deacons of the church to get involved in the community and get the message out to these young brothers because—trust me—there are many who do want to hear it. It's time for our women with great influence to talk to our young females and teach them the true definition of self-respect and being a boss. We can't sit around waiting for the next Dr. Martin Luther King Jr. or Brother Malcolm X to arrive on the scene. It's time for us all to play our part and come together as one and quit sitting around waiting for the next big thing to happen. Be the next big thing.

Teach our youth to utilize the internet for their benefit. All it takes is a group of young brothers and sisters to produce a YouTube video about their community and the need for a library, boys and girls club, new uniforms for sports, etc. and eventually someone will get involved (the mayor, a Congressman, an entertainer, an athlete, etc.). It can happen. Teach your kids some marketing skills which will benefit the community as a whole. Encourage them to read more instead of playing video games all day and talking on the phone. Instead of driving everywhere, start walking more often. It'll get some blood pumping into your veins.

Let's start eating healthy and teach our kids to also eat healthy. Take care of your body and your body will take care of you. Break those chains off your mind which have held you in bondage for so many years. Our great-grandparents and their ancestors were programmed at early ages and those bondages have been passed down to us. A lot of the things we have been taught were meant to destroy us and keep us at odds with each other. If you return to the root of your knowledge and learning you will find the solution to your problems. It's time to break the chains and be reprogrammed so that our minds can properly function. We have those same viruses you find in computers, in our minds. If you allow the wrong messages into your mind they may contain viruses that can mess up your entire computer (your brain).

Watch what you allow into your thought process. It can have a negative effect on not only those around you, but your children also. They are quick to pick up new habits and things from adults. Life is precious. Respect life and all that it has to offer. No one said life would be a cakewalk. It's not meant to be. It's meant to be the greatest teacher while you are here on earth. What you learn can be beneficial for generations to come if you apply yourself and think that far into the future. The key has been given to you. It's on you to unlock the chains. If you are mentally strong enough you may be able to break them!

Part 5

REWRITING MY LEGACY

CHAPTER 12

Rewriting My Legacy: 31-Day Journal

If you've made it this far, this is the time to smile and give yourself the credit you deserve. How do you feel? Are you more at peace? Do you view life and others in a more positive aspect? Remember, earlier in the book you went through the 31-day reprogramming of the mind challenge. This is the second installment to that challenge. This is your opportunity to rewrite your legacy. Rewriting your legacy is your chance to make amends with yourself. This is your chance to forgive yourself and move forward.

"How do you do this?" Through journaling. A journal is a record of your life, what you have experienced, your emotions, feelings, etc. By keeping a journal, you can always go back, reread your thoughts for the day and reflect. Your journal also tracks your growth and maturity. I want you to try this: Go back and reread your 31-day program. For each day you read, write a page-length entry in the journal provided in this section of the book. If you choose to write about something more interesting or not related to the 31-day program, do that also. But for the next 31-days get familiar with writing in your journal.

This is meant to encourage you to go out and purchase a dairy or composition notebook and continue journaling after you complete this book. If you prefer, you can keep your journal entries in this book, or you can simply tear them out for your use (especially if you intend to share the book with others). A simple diary or journal can be purchased for as little as 99 cents. However, if you desire a more formal one, it may cost you more. Are you up for the challenge? Are you ready to rewrite your legacy? Let's go!

Helpful Tips Needed for Journal Writing:

1. Write your true emotions and feelings.

2. Are you writing about yourself, a person, place or thing?

3. How do you feel?

4. Where are you? (Time, place, who, what, when, where, why, how)

5. If you are writing about something you read, what was your interpretation? What did you learn? How can you apply it to your life?

* Be sure to always date your journal entries and include a (where) and (place). This helps you remember and reflect on that day more effectively.

31-DAY JOURNAL

JOURNAL ENTRY

Day: 1

Mood: _____ Date: _____

(ex. happy, sad, angry, depressed, afraid, etc.)

Level of Mood: _____ Place: _____

(1 to 10, 10 being the highest)

_____

_____

_____

_____

_____

_____

_____

_____

_____

_____

_____

_____

_____

_____

Time Completed: _____

Mood After Completed: _____

Level of Mood After Completed: _____

JOURNAL ENTRY

Day: 2

Mood: _____ Date: _____

    (ex. happy, sad, angry, depressed, afraid, etc.)

Level of Mood: _____ Place: _____

    (1 to 10, 10 being the highest)

_____

_____

_____

_____

_____

_____

_____

_____

_____

_____

_____

_____

_____

_____

Time Completed: _____

Mood After Completed: _____

Level of Mood After Completed: _____

JOURNAL ENTRY

Day: 3

Mood: _____ **Date:** _____
    (ex. happy, sad, angry, depressed, afraid, etc.)

Level of Mood: _____ **Place:** _____
    (1 to 10, 10 being the highest)

_____

_____

_____

_____

_____

_____

_____

_____

_____

_____

_____

_____

_____

_____

_____

Time Completed: _____

Mood After Completed: _____

Level of Mood After Completed: _____

JOURNAL ENTRY

Day: 4

Mood: _____ **Date:** _____
    (ex. happy, sad, angry, depressed, afraid, etc.)

Level of Mood: _____ **Place:** _____
    (1 to 10, 10 being the highest)

_____

_____

_____

_____

_____

_____

_____

_____

_____

_____

_____

_____

_____

_____

Time Completed: _____

Mood After Completed: _____

Level of Mood After Completed: _____

JOURNAL ENTRY

Day: 5

Mood: _____ Date: _____

    (ex. happy, sad, angry, depressed, afraid, etc.)

Level of Mood: _____ Place: _____

    (1 to 10, 10 being the highest)

_____

_____

_____

_____

_____

_____

_____

_____

_____

_____

_____

_____

_____

_____

_____

Time Completed: _____

Mood After Completed: _____

Level of Mood After Completed: _____

JOURNAL ENTRY

Day: 6

Mood: _____ **Date:** _____

    (ex. happy, sad, angry, depressed, afraid, etc.)

Level of Mood: _____ **Place:** _____

    (1 to 10, 10 being the highest)

_____

_____

_____

_____

_____

_____

_____

_____

_____

_____

_____

_____

_____

_____

_____

Time Completed: _____

Mood After Completed: _____

Level of Mood After Completed: _____

JOURNAL ENTRY

Day: 7

Mood: _____ Date: _____

    (ex. happy, sad, angry, depressed, afraid, etc.)

Level of Mood: _____ Place: _____

    (1 to 10, 10 being the highest)

_____

_____

_____

_____

_____

_____

_____

_____

_____

_____

_____

_____

_____

_____

_____

Time Completed: _____

Mood After Completed: _____

Level of Mood After Completed: _____

JOURNAL ENTRY

Day: 8

Mood: _____ Date: _____

(ex. happy, sad, angry, depressed, afraid, etc.)

Level of Mood: _____ Place: _____

(1 to 10, 10 being the highest)

_____

_____

_____

_____

_____

_____

_____

_____

_____

_____

_____

_____

_____

_____

_____

_____

Time Completed: _____

Mood After Completed: _____

Level of Mood After Completed: _____

JOURNAL ENTRY

Day: 9

Mood: _____ Date: _____

    (ex. happy, sad, angry, depressed, afraid, etc.)

Level of Mood: _____ Place: _____

    (1 to 10, 10 being the highest)

_____

_____

_____

_____

_____

_____

_____

_____

_____

_____

_____

_____

_____

_____

_____

Time Completed: _____

Mood After Completed: _____

Level of Mood After Completed: _____

JOURNAL ENTRY

Day: 10

Mood: _____ **Date:** _____

    (ex. happy, sad, angry, depressed, afraid, etc.)

Level of Mood: _____ **Place:** _____

    (1 to 10, 10 being the highest)

_____

_____

_____

_____

_____

_____

_____

_____

_____

_____

_____

_____

_____

_____

Time Completed: _____

Mood After Completed: _____

Level of Mood After Completed: _____

JOURNAL ENTRY

Day: 11

Mood: _____ Date: _____

    (ex. happy, sad, angry, depressed, afraid, etc.)

Level of Mood: _____ Place: _____

    (1 to 10, 10 being the highest)

_____

_____

_____

_____

_____

_____

_____

_____

_____

_____

_____

_____

_____

_____

_____

Time Completed: _____

Mood After Completed: _____

Level of Mood After Completed: _____

JOURNAL ENTRY

Day: 12

Mood: _____ Date: _____

     (ex. happy, sad, angry, depressed, afraid, etc.)

Level of Mood: _____ Place: _____

     (1 to 10, 10 being the highest)

_____

_____

_____

_____

_____

_____

_____

_____

_____

_____

_____

_____

_____

_____

_____

Time Completed: _____

Mood After Completed: _____

Level of Mood After Completed: _____

JOURNAL ENTRY

Day: 13

Mood: _____ Date: _____

   (ex. happy, sad, angry, depressed, afraid, etc.)

Level of Mood: _____ Place: _____

   (1 to 10, 10 being the highest)

_____

_____

_____

_____

_____

_____

_____

_____

_____

_____

_____

_____

_____

_____

_____

Time Completed: _____

Mood After Completed: _____

Level of Mood After Completed: _____

JOURNAL ENTRY

Day: 14

Mood: _____ Date: _____

    (ex. happy, sad, angry, depressed, afraid, etc.)

Level of Mood: _____ Place: _____

    (1 to 10, 10 being the highest)

_____

_____

_____

_____

_____

_____

_____

_____

_____

_____

_____

_____

_____

_____

_____

Time Completed: _____

Mood After Completed: _____

Level of Mood After Completed: _____

JOURNAL ENTRY

Day: 15

Mood: _____ Date: _____

    (ex. happy, sad, angry, depressed, afraid, etc.)

Level of Mood: _____ Place: _____

    (1 to 10, 10 being the highest)

_____

_____

_____

_____

_____

_____

_____

_____

_____

_____

_____

_____

_____

_____

_____

Time Completed: _____

Mood After Completed: _____

Level of Mood After Completed: _____

JOURNAL ENTRY

Day: 16

Mood: _____ **Date:** _____
    (ex. happy, sad, angry, depressed, afraid, etc.)

Level of Mood: _____ **Place:** _____
    (1 to 10, 10 being the highest)

_____

_____

_____

_____

_____

_____

_____

_____

_____

_____

_____

_____

_____

_____

_____

Time Completed: _____

Mood After Completed: _____

Level of Mood After Completed: _____

JOURNAL ENTRY

Day: 17

Mood: _____ Date: _____
    (ex. happy, sad, angry, depressed, afraid, etc.)

Level of Mood: _____ Place: _____
    (1 to 10, 10 being the highest)

_____

_____

_____

_____

_____

_____

_____

_____

_____

_____

_____

_____

_____

_____

_____

Time Completed: _____

Mood After Completed: _____

Level of Mood After Completed: _____

JOURNAL ENTRY

Day: 18

Mood: _____ Date: _____

    (ex. happy, sad, angry, depressed, afraid, etc.)

Level of Mood: _____ Place: _____

    (1 to 10, 10 being the highest)

_____

_____

_____

_____

_____

_____

_____

_____

_____

_____

_____

_____

_____

_____

_____

Time Completed: _____

Mood After Completed: _____

Level of Mood After Completed: _____

JOURNAL ENTRY

Day: 19

Mood: _____ Date: _____

(ex. happy, sad, angry, depressed, afraid, etc.)

Level of Mood: _____ Place: _____

(1 to 10, 10 being the highest)

_____

_____

_____

_____

_____

_____

_____

_____

_____

_____

_____

_____

_____

_____

_____

Time Completed: _____

Mood After Completed: _____

Level of Mood After Completed: _____

JOURNAL ENTRY

Day: 20

Mood: _____ Date: _____

    (ex. happy, sad, angry, depressed, afraid, etc.)

Level of Mood: _____ Place: _____

    (1 to 10, 10 being the highest)

_____

_____

_____

_____

_____

_____

_____

_____

_____

_____

_____

_____

_____

_____

_____

Time Completed: _____

Mood After Completed: _____

Level of Mood After Completed: _____

JOURNAL ENTRY

Day: 21

Mood: _____ Date: _____

(ex. happy, sad, angry, depressed, afraid, etc.)

Level of Mood: _____ Place: _____

(1 to 10, 10 being the highest)

_____

_____

_____

_____

_____

_____

_____

_____

_____

_____

_____

_____

_____

_____

_____

_____

Time Completed: _____

Mood After Completed: _____

Level of Mood After Completed: _____

JOURNAL ENTRY

Day: 22

Mood: _____ Date: _____
   (ex. happy, sad, angry, depressed, afraid, etc.)

Level of Mood: _____ Place: _____
   (1 to 10, 10 being the highest)

_____

_____

_____

_____

_____

_____

_____

_____

_____

_____

_____

_____

_____

_____

_____

Time Completed: _____

Mood After Completed: _____

Level of Mood After Completed: _____

JOURNAL ENTRY

Day: 23

Mood: _____ Date: _____
     (ex. happy, sad, angry, depressed, afraid, etc.)

Level of Mood: _____ Place: _____
     (1 to 10, 10 being the highest)

_____

_____

_____

_____

_____

_____

_____

_____

_____

_____

_____

_____

_____

_____

_____

Time Completed: _____

Mood After Completed: _____

Level of Mood After Completed: _____

JOURNAL ENTRY

Day: 24

Mood: _____ Date: _____

    (ex. happy, sad, angry, depressed, afraid, etc.)

Level of Mood: _____ Place: _____

    (1 to 10, 10 being the highest)

_____

_____

_____

_____

_____

_____

_____

_____

_____

_____

_____

_____

_____

_____

_____

Time Completed: _____

Mood After Completed: _____

Level of Mood After Completed: _____

JOURNAL ENTRY

Day: 25

Mood: _____ Date: _____

    (ex. happy, sad, angry, depressed, afraid, etc.)

Level of Mood: _____ Place: _____

    (1 to 10, 10 being the highest)

_____

_____

_____

_____

_____

_____

_____

_____

_____

_____

_____

_____

_____

_____

_____

Time Completed: _____

Mood After Completed: _____

Level of Mood After Completed: _____

JOURNAL ENTRY

Day: 26

Mood: _____ **Date:** _____
    (ex. happy, sad, angry, depressed, afraid, etc.)

Level of Mood: _____ **Place:** _____
    (1 to 10, 10 being the highest)

_____

_____

_____

_____

_____

_____

_____

_____

_____

_____

_____

_____

_____

_____

_____

Time Completed: _____

Mood After Completed: _____

Level of Mood After Completed: _____

JOURNAL ENTRY

Day: 27

Mood: _____ Date: _____

(ex. happy, sad, angry, depressed, afraid, etc.)

Level of Mood: _____ Place: _____

(1 to 10, 10 being the highest)

_____

_____

_____

_____

_____

_____

_____

_____

_____

_____

_____

_____

_____

_____

_____

_____

Time Completed: _____

Mood After Completed: _____

Level of Mood After Completed: _____

JOURNAL ENTRY

Day: 28

Mood: _____ Date: _____

  (ex. happy, sad, angry, depressed, afraid, etc.)

Level of Mood: _____ Place: _____

  (1 to 10, 10 being the highest)

_____

_____

_____

_____

_____

_____

_____

_____

_____

_____

_____

_____

_____

_____

_____

Time Completed: _____

Mood After Completed: _____

Level of Mood After Completed: _____

JOURNAL ENTRY

Day: 29

Mood: _____ Date: _____

    (ex. happy, sad, angry, depressed, afraid, etc.)

Level of Mood: _____ Place: _____

    (1 to 10, 10 being the highest)

_____

_____

_____

_____

_____

_____

_____

_____

_____

_____

_____

_____

_____

_____

_____

_____

Time Completed: _____

Mood After Completed: _____

Level of Mood After Completed: _____

JOURNAL ENTRY

Day: 30

Mood: _____ Date: _____

    (ex. happy, sad, angry, depressed, afraid, etc.)

Level of Mood: _____ Place: _____

    (1 to 10, 10 being the highest)

_____

_____

_____

_____

_____

_____

_____

_____

_____

_____

_____

_____

_____

_____

_____

Time Completed: _____

Mood After Completed: _____

Level of Mood After Completed: _____

JOURNAL ENTRY

Day: 31

Mood: _____ Date: _____

    (ex. happy, sad, angry, depressed, afraid, etc.)

Level of Mood: _____ Place: _____

    (1 to 10, 10 being the highest)

_____

_____

_____

_____

_____

_____

_____

_____

_____

_____

_____

_____

_____

_____

_____

Time Completed: _____

Mood After Completed: _____

Level of Mood After Completed: _____

Meet the Author

Name: Mr. Phillip D. White

Age: 36 years old

Hometown: Muncie, Indiana (Indianapolis, Indiana)

Mr. P. D. White knows what it's like to be free, enjoying the luxury of freedom. He also knows what it feels like to be incarcerated; not just physically but mentally, emotionally, spiritually and financially. At the age of twelve Mr. White was going to school, selling drugs, to help his mother pay bills. He was the eldest of three siblings and considered himself "the man of the house."

By the age of thirteen Mr. White was in and out of juvenile halls for a number of charges, truancy being his most common offense. It was either education or keep the lights on. At the age of eighteen he'd managed to become a successful drug dealer who built his lifestyle by destroying the lives of others. It wasn't until his first child was born a year later that Mr. White would understand the true meaning of responsibility and manhood. Unfortunately, over the next years Mr. White would be shot; had to deal with the tragedy of his son being hit and paralyzed from hit and run accident by an intoxicated driver; and lose his freedom from a drug indictment.

At twenty-three years old he would find himself in prison; alone, confused but not yet broken. After a three-year stint he was released. Free again. He knew he had to change, not just for himself, but for his first son, second son and daughter. He now had three children. After a short-lived career in the music industry, he signed with Naptown Records—a label owned by comedian Mike Epps—which included nights of partying, sex, money, drug use, cars, clothing and all that came with the lifestyle of being a rap artist. Once again, Mr. White found himself in prison. But this time there would be no slap on the wrist. He was charged with first-degree murder.

It was during this time he discovered himself; his worth, his purpose in life, and his purpose on earth: to serve God. As Mr. White began to serve God, he also found himself enjoying the pleasure of serving others. After obtaining his GED, getting baptized and vowing never to sell or use drugs again, Mr. White began to encourage other incarcerated young brothers to do the same. In no time he found himself being a "Big Brother" figure to many and giving advice when asked. And while learning the Bible for the first time in his life, he began to hold Bible study and also taught others. It was then that he began to see the young brothers end their thuggish ways, enroll into school, get baptized and vow to also change their lives. Mr. P. D. White was finally blessed to know his true purpose for not only his life but for being incarcerated.

While being incarcerated Mr. White enrolled in college where he's working on earning his AA Degree in Psychology He has participated in and completed programs and classes such as Toastmasters, NA, AA, Anger Management, Kairos; book clubs, creative writing, poetry and writing classes; Actor's Gang (a course/group ran by actor Tim Robbins), 10P Life empowerment group (ran by Samual Brown), Men's Group, Prep Insight; as well as earning his degree/certification for Hazardous Material Safety, Louder Than a Bomb Poetry Slam, Substance Awareness, student teaching and mentoring and a host of other achievements. To add to his long list of accomplishments, Mr. White is the first prisoner to propose and successfully start a newspaper at CSP-SAC (New Folsom) called "Concrete Rose." Not stopping there, he also proposed the start of a self-help group called "Peer Positive Group Leadership" for mentally ill prisoners. This group is still in operation. Upon his transfer to CMC East men's facility, he now runs and facilitates his own self-help class called "Inner Strength Course" where he teaches other prisoners how to reprogram their way of thinking, embrace insight and remorse for their crimes, and learn self-discipline.

Mr. P. D. White has given lectures while incarcerated. The guests included law students enrolled in Criminal Justice programs at Sacramento State College. These students were also in the company of their Professor, Dr. Ernest Uwazie, an honorable law professor from which Mr. White has been honored to receive therapy sessions in rehabilitation. Dr. Uwazie is a Professor of Criminal Justice and Restorative Justice and facilitates several seminars on Victim-Offender Mediation. It was these classes that assisted Mr. White in coming to grips with the reality of his crime and the grief he caused to others due to his actions.

Mr. P. D. White is the author of *"Concrete Walls & Steel Bars: The New Willie Lynch."* This is a self-help book and journal that not only motivates its readers but also encourages them to reprogram their minds and train their thoughts through reflection and journaling. It teaches them the skills needed to unlock the chains and shackles many may find their minds imprisoned within. He dedicates his time to changing his negative circumstances into positive steppingstones which can be used to help others.

Mr. P. D. White is focused on rebuilding the communities he once destroyed. He also mentors and tutors youth prisoners so they, too, can obtain a GED and hopefully one day enroll into college if that is their desire. He encourages those around him to focus on change and not allow their past to define their future. His mission is to give back to those he hurt purposely or by mistake. The new generation is the future and Mr. White is devoted to teaching them true morals, values, integrity and how to be productive assets to their family and community.

The New Willie Lynch   Concrete Walls & Steel Bars
Mr. P. D. White

Although Mr. White was shackled by dealing drugs, drug use, money, violence, genocide, unprotected sex and other false-negative things, he has now found the key which was buried deep within him. He has managed to unlock the chains. Mr. White believes in being a positive influence. He knows better than anyone that "it takes a minute to make a mistake and a lifetime to fix the mistake." He also believes that "no sin is greater than the next," and everyone deserves a second, third and even fourth chance.

Mr. P. D. White is engaged to be married and contributes his time to being a better fiancé, friend, provider, listener and helper to his beautiful woman. He is dedicated to being continually productive and positive for the sake of God, his mother, his sister, brother, grandmother, children, niece, cousins, godmother, friends other relatives, family members and the community that continues to embrace him through all his adversity.

Mr. P. D. White resides in California with his fiancé and beautiful step-children where they enjoy the luxury of love, joy, peace and happiness.

Facebook: Phillip D White

Twitter: @Concretewalls1

Instagram: Concretewallsand steelbars

Email: Concretewallsandsteelbars@Gmail.com

RESOURCES

65 Top Websites to Announce Your Book for Free

https://savvybookwriters.wordpress.com

Affordable Housing

www.voa.org/housing

Volunteers of America

1660 Duke Street

Alexandria, VA 22314

Phone: (703) 341-5000

African-American History Books

www.blackbooksdirect.com/history/html

Best African-American History Books

https://www.amazon.com

American Red Cross National Headquarters

2025 E. Street, NW

Washington, DC 20006

Phone: 1- (800) RED CROSS (1-800-733-2767)

http:/www.redcross.org

Birth Certificates

(Check with your local County Clerk Office)

Boys and Girls Club of America Headquarters

bgca.org/pages/contact.aspx

Email general inquiries to: info@bgca.org

Locations: National Headquarters/Service Center/Overseas Military Youth

Centers/Clubs

1275 Peachtree Street, NE

Atlanta, GA 30309-3506

Phone: (404) 487-5700

Email general inquiries to: info@bgca.org

Office of Government Relations

1707 L Street, NW, Suite 670

Washington, DC 20037

Phone: (202) 507-6670

Chicago Service Center

1590 Wilkening Road

Schaumberg, IL 60173

Phone: (847) 490-5220

Civil Rights Litigation Group

1391 Speer Blvd. Suite 705

Denver, CO 80204

Phone: (720) 515-6165

Fax: (303) 534-1949

www.rightslitigation.com

Dallas Service Center

2107 N. Collins Blvd.

Richardson, TX 75080

Phone: (972) 581-2360

Domestic Abuse/Battered Women

www.thehotline.org

Phone: 1-(800) 799-SAFE (1-800-799-7233) (Bilingual advocates on hand)

Women Helping Battered Women

www.whbw.org

Phone: 1-(800) ABUSE95 (1-800-228-7395)

Drug Abuse

SAMHA (Substance Abuse and Mental Illness Administration)

Phone: 1-(800) 662- HELP (1-800-662-4357)

Felon-Friendly Employers (Companies that hire felons):

Aamco	www.aamco.com
Ace Hardware	www.acehardware.com
Allied Van Lines	www.allied.com
American Greetings	www.americangreetings.com
Andersen Windows	www.andersenwindows.com
Apple, Inc.	www.apple.com
Aramark	www.aramark.com
AT&T	https://www.att.com
Avon Products	https://www.avon.com
Baskin-Robbins	https://www.baskinrobbins.com
Bed, Bath and Beyond	www.bedbathandbeyond.com
Black & Decker	www.blackanddecker.com
Blue Cross and Blue Shield Association	www.bcbs.com
Braum's, Inc.	www.braums.com
Bridgestone Tires	www.bridgestonetire.com
Buffalo Wild Wings	www.buffalowildwings.com
Campbell's Soup	www.campbells.com
Canon	www.usa.canon.com
Carl's Jr.	www.carlsjr.com
Caterpillar, Inc.	www.caterpillar.com
CDW	https://www.cdw.com
Chili's	www.chilis.com
Chipotle	www.chipotle.com

Cintas	www.cintas.com/careers
Community Education Centers	(check your local centers)
ConAgra Foods	www.conagrafoods.com
Dairy Queen	www.dairyqueen.com
Delta Faucet	https://www.deltafaucet.com
Denny's	www.dennys.com
Dole Food Company	www.dole.com
Dollar Rent-a-Car	https://www.dollar.com
Dollar Tree	www.dollartree.com
Dr. Pepper	www.drpepper.com
Dunlop Tires	www.dunloptires.com
Dunkin' Donuts	www.dunkindonuts.com
DuPont	www.dupont.com
Duracell	https://www.duracell.com
Epson	www.epson.com
ERMCO, Inc.	www.ermco.com
Family Dollar	https://familydollar.com
Firestone Auto Care	www.firestone.com
Pilot Flying J	www.jobs.pilotflyingj.com
Fruit of the Loom	www.fruitoftheloom.com
Fuji Film	www.fujifilm.com
General Electric	www.ge.com
General Mills	www.generalmills.com
Georgia-Pacific	www.gp.com/careers

Goodwill	www.goodwill.org
Grainger	https://jobs.grainger.com
Greyhound Bus	www.greyhound.com
Hanes	www.hanes.com
Hilton Hotels	www.hiltonworldwide.com
Home Depot	www.homedepot.com
IBM	http://www-03.ibm.com/employment
In-N-Out-Burger	www.in-n-out.com
Jack-in-the-Box	www.jackinthebox.com
K-Mart	www.kmart.com
Kelly Moore Paints	www.kellymoore.com
Kentucky Fried Chicken	https://jobs.kfc.com
Kohl's	www.kohls.com
Kraft Foods	

www.kraftheinzcompany.com/careers

Kroger	www.kroger.com
Long Horn Steak House	www.longhornsteakhouse.com
Lowe's	https://careers.lowes.com
LSG Sky Chefs	www.lsgskychefs.com
McDonald's	http://mcdonalds.jobs
Men's Wearhouse	www.menswearhouse.com
Metals USA	www.metalsusa.com
Miller Brewing Company	http://www.millercoors.com
Motorola	http://motorolacareers.com
The New York Times	http://nytimes.com/section/jobs

Olive Garden	http://olivegarden.com/careers
PepsiCo	www.pepsicojobs.com
Phillip Morris Inc.	
	http://www.pmi.com/eng/careers/Pages/jobs.aspx
Pilgrim's	www.pilgrims.com
Red Lobster	https://www.redlobster.com/work-with-us
Red Robin	http:www.redrobinpa.com/careers
Safeway	www.safeway.com/careers
Trader Joes	www.traderjoes.com/careers
Tyson Foods	www.tysonfoods.com
U-Haul	http://www.jobs.uhaul.com
US Steel Corporation	http://www.ussteel.com
Volunteers of America	https://www.voa.org/careers
Walgreens	https://jobs.walgreens.com
Wendy's	https://www.wendys.com/en-us/careers

Free Books for Children

www.imaginationlibrary.com

Free Books

Gang Prevention

National Crime Prevention Council

(Strategy: Gang Prevention through Community Intervention with

High-Risk Youth)

www.ncpc.org

2614 Chapel Lake Drive Suite B

Gambrills, MD 21054

Phone: (443) 292-4565

Goodwill Industries International, Inc.

15810 Indianola Drive

Rockville, MD 20855

Phone: 1-(800) GOODWILL (1-800-466-3955)

Email: contactus@goodwill.org

Government Assistance Information

Phone: 1-(844) USA-GOV1 (1-844-872-4681)

www.usa.gov/benefits-grants-loans

HIV/AIDS Federal Facts and Prevention Programs

https:/www.aids.gov

http://aidsinfo.nih.gov

http://mayoclinic.org/diseases-conditions/hiv-aids

Homeless Shelters

www.homelessshelterdirectory.org

www.jobsthathirefelons.org

Resume Writing – 101 Best Resumes

https://www.amazon.com

How To Write a Resume

http://www.monster.com/career-advice

Ten Top Resume Writing Books

http://resume-blogspot.com/2013/06/ten-to-resume-writing-books.html

Salvation Army

615 Slaters Lane

Alexandria, VA 22313

Phone: (703) 684-5500

http://www.salvationarmyusa.org

Small Business Association

www.sba.gov

Social Security Administration

www.ssa.gov

U.S. Copyright Office

101 Independence Avenue, SE

Washington, DC 20559-6000

http://www.copyright.gov

U.S. Small Business Administration

409 3rd Street, SW

Washington, DC 20416

Phone: SBA Answer Desk 1-(800) 827-5722

Footnotes and Sources

Chapter 1:

[1]New King James Version Bible

[2]A.M.E. Church massacre in Charleston, SC which took the lives of nine churchgoers.

Chapter 2:

[1]Bureau of Justice Statistics, National Prisoner Statistics Program, 1978-2013-U.S. Department
 of Justice.

[2]National Corrections Reporting Program, 2012: and survey of inmates in state and federal
  correctional facilities, 2004-U.S. Department of Justice.

[3]Bureau of Justice Statistics, National Prisoners Statistics Program and National Corrections
  Reporting Program, 2012: and survey of inmates in state correctional facilities, 2004.

Chapter 3:

[1]U.S. Census Bureau, children's living arrangements and characteristics: March 2011, table c8, Washington, DC: 2011.

[2]U.S. Department of Health and Human Services: asep issue brief: information on poverty and income statistics, September 12, 2012, http://aspe.hsp/12/povertyandincomeest/ib.shtml.

[3]Hoffman, John P. "Journal of Marriage and Family," 64, (May 2002): 314-330.

[4]The Lancet - January 25, 2003, gunilla ringback weitoft, M.D. Centre for Epidemiology, The National Board of Health and Welfare, www.webmd.com/baby/news/20030123/absent-parent-doubles-child-suicide-risk.

[5]Osbourne, C. and Mclanahan S. "Journal of Marriage and Family," 69, (2007):1065-1083.

[6]Kruk, Edward Ph.D. "The vital importance of paternal presence in children's lives," May 23,

2012, www.psychologytoday.com/blog/co-parenting-

afterdivorce/201205/father-absence-

father-deficit-father-hunger.

[7]Stephen Demuth and Susan L. Brown "Family Structure, family

process & adolescent

delinquency," http:/www.Family Facts.Org/Briefs/26/marriage-

and-family as deterrents-from-

delinquency-violence-and-crime.

[8]2013-High School Longitudinal Study of 2009 (hsls:09).

Made in the USA
Columbia, SC
08 January 2024

29370930R00171